Aseema: A Journey Beyond Boundaries

DILBUR PARAKH

Illustrated by Ashish Gaikwad and Vicky Thorat

ISBN 979-8-89067-844-7

Dedication

To my parents

To the children of Aseema, and

To the One who makes everything possible

Endorsements

Aseema is synonymous with BNP Paribas, India's CSR journey. As one of its oldest philanthropic partners, I have closely witnessed Dilbur and her team of passionate professionals elevate the quality of educational interventions among children from marginalised backgrounds. This book depicts her inspiring journey and illustrates the deep impact Aseema has in delivering change through education.

– Alain Papiasse
Chairman, Advisory Board, BNP Paribas India Foundation

* * *

I met Dilbur Parakh in Geneva in the 1990s when she was working for the ICJ and I was Chef de Cabinet to the High Commissioner for Human Rights. We spent quality time together. She knew her destiny would take her back to India. I was with her when she took that very difficult decision to resign and return home. A few months later, I did the same, but unlike Dilbur, I re-joined the Indian Foreign Service. She had no job waiting for her back home. Dilbur is a person of extraordinary compassion, courage, and vision. Aseema was her creation, and this book is her life story. As the caption says: *"This book tells the story of Aseema, and the woman who built it—student by student, school by school"*. It adds: *"Aseema. Like the name suggests, this story has no end. But it has a beginning. And this book attempts to tell it"*. I am privileged to extend my wholehearted endorsement to 'Aseema—A Journey beyond Boundaries'.

After 2014, I was proud to be a member of Aseema's Advisory Board. I witnessed how education can transform and empower children. Later, I worked hard to raise funds for the many projects, which needed support.

I travelled to Igatpuri for its inauguration. It was a revelation. This remote corner of Maharashtra has been revolutionised by quality education for tribal children. It provides valuable lessons on how Dilbur's vision and determination overcame every formidable challenge to her efforts to change the lives of her students.

This book is a must-read. It provides hope for India's future and demonstrates the resilience of the poor and marginalised in determining and shaping a new future with 'Aseema'. May Aseema's limitless journey be blessed and may it continue its noble mission.

– Ambassador Bhaswati Mukherjee
Diplomat, Author, and President of India Habitat Centre

* * *

"I am delighted to endorse Dilbur Parakh's book—"*Aseema: A Journey Beyond Boundaries*", a compelling narrative that encapsulates the 25-year odyssey of Aseema, an organisation that has been a beacon of hope for impoverished children in India. Having supported Aseema for the past decade, I am aware of the profound impact the NGO has had on the lives of countless children, providing them with not just education, but a chance to dream and aspire for a better future. This book is not just a chronicle of Aseema's remarkable journey, but also a testament to the indomitable human spirit and the transformative power of compassion and determination. I urge everyone to read this inspiring book, as it not only sheds light on the incredible work that Aseema does but also serves as a clarion call for each one of us to do what we can to make a difference in the world. Together, we can create a brighter future for all."

– Boman Rustom Irani
Chairman and Managing Director, Rustomjee Group

* * *

It gives me great pleasure to recommend Dilbur's book, *Aseema: A Journey Beyond Boundaries*. I have known her and Aseema for more than 14 years. I first encountered Aseema when our team was in India to make the film, *Slumdog Millionaire*, which went on to win several awards in 2009, including eight Oscars and seven BAFTAs. The credit for that success belongs to some extent to Aseema's children, who performed in the film. Since those days, I have kept in touch with Dilbur and Aseema and have been greatly impressed to see them thrive in so many ways.

Their extraordinary work is always accomplished with great skill and humility. I am delighted that Dilbur has chosen to write Aseema's story. It deserves to be widely read, and Aseema deserves to be equally widely supported.

– Danny Boyle
Film director and producer

* * *

I have been privileged to know Dilbur Parakh for more than 40 years and I am therefore delighted to recommend this un-put-downable book that she has authored.

In the 1990s, Dilbur, a bright and energetic young lawyer, held a responsible position in the Geneva-based human rights organisation—the International Commission of Jurists. However, after a few years, she chose to give up her job in order to fulfil her life's laudable ambition: to work for the poor and needy in India! With a few close friends, Dilbur then set up Aseema, a public charitable trust for the education of underprivileged children—and since then she has never looked back.

Noted historian Will Durant had described education as "the technique of transmitting civilisation", and at about the same time H.G. Wells, the most prolific writer of the twentieth century had proclaimed that "human history has become more and more a race between education and catastrophe".

Dilbur's captivating memoir, titled *Aseema: A Journey Beyond Boundaries* (*Aseema* in Sanskrit means "limitless and without boundaries") unveils the story, brick-by-brick, of a grassroots initiative that has helped to revolutionise education; but, more importantly, it has also helped to uplift the lives of several thousand children in marginalised communities, averting the catastrophe about which HGW had warned!

– Fali S. Nariman
Jurist and Honorary Member, International Commission of Jurists (ICJ)

* * *

I met Dilbur in Mumbai in the 1990s, as a fellow disciple of Sri Sri Paramahansa Yogananda. We met every week for group meditation sessions. She came across as a very sweet, gentle, humble person. I had no idea about her achievements until I interacted with her and got to know more about her life and activities. Today, we share a deep bond of love and friendship.

I have been a witness to Aseema's growth and achievements over the years. The journey has been a difficult one. Yet, Dilbur's perseverance, determination, dedication, commitment, loyalty, and love for her students, teachers, and all her staff have helped Aseema to be recognized as a world-renowned NGO today. The word, "impossible" has no place in Dilbur's dictionary!

Dilbur's book, "Aseema: A Journey Beyond Boundaries" is a must-read for every person who has dreams and goals. Each one of us has the potential. All we need to do is believe in ourselves and forge ahead with courage, faith, strength, hope, and determination. Dilbur tapped her talent and potential to the fullest. Her heart beats for all, irrespective of caste, colour, race, and creed. Her desire and aspiration to "keep on keeping on" and giving of herself are limitless, never-ending like her creation, "Aseema"!

These words of Sri Sri Paramahansa Yogananda aptly describe Dilbur's all-fulfilling life:

"In being of spiritual, mental, and material service to others, you will find your own needs fulfilled. As you forget self in service to others, you will find that, without seeking it, your own cup of happiness will be full."

I am truly honoured to endorse this very inspiring and engrossing book. Kudos, dear friend– may your tribe increase!

– Gita Pai
Paramahansa Yogananda Sadhnalaya, Igatpuri

* * *

Our ability to assist the Aseema online worldwide auction of outstanding student artworks was a wonderful honour. We were so moved when we learned about the schools and how Dilbur Parakh built this amazing institution. Aseema goes above and beyond in its dedication and generosity to underprivileged kids. Dilbur's extraordinary leadership and her team's unwavering spirit of commitment and kindness are the epitome of giving back and improving the world.

– Grace Cho
Founder and CEO, Artrepreneur.com

* * *

The story of the first 25 years of Aseema is a captivating story that is a must-read for anyone interested in visionary social entrepreneurship, value-based innovative new educational paradigms, the values of truth, simplicity, humility, hard work, and love for all humanity in action, innovative growth strategies for non-profit organisations, courage, and dedication to a vision.

Enjoy and be inspired!

– Jerry Wind
The Lauder Professor Emeritus, The Wharton School
Founder of the Lauder Institute and Wharton Executive MBA Program
Co-founder of Reimagine Education Global Competition
Co-founder Reichman University

* * *

I am pleased to extend my endorsement for the book *Aseema: A Journey Beyond Boundaries* penned by Dilbur Parakh, founder of Aseema.

The book vividly encapsulates the incredible 25-year journey of Aseema, chronicling both the uphill battles and the remarkable milestones achieved under the visionary leadership of Dilbur. As a proud partner, we at Societe Generale have had the privilege of being part of this transformative journey in youth education for almost a decade. We thank Aseema for their boundless efforts and strong determination to open the door to opportunities for underprivileged children in Mumbai and Igatpuri. This book offers a collection of inspiring stories, including a glimpse into Dilbur's personal journey from having a distinguished international career to walking an unconventional path to uplift and empower kids from the neighbourhood, which will motivate aspiring social entrepreneurs.

– Dr Katan Hirachand
Chief Executive and Chief Country Officer,
Societe Generale Bank, India

* * *

In my many years of working with the children of the world, I have witnessed firsthand the life-changing potency of education, not just in India, but around the world. That is why I am so moved by Dilbur and the Aseema stories.

This enthralling journey began in the heart of bustling Mumbai, propelled by a firm belief in the transforming power of education. Aseema's tenacity and adaptability drove it beyond Mumbai, introducing education to tribal villages and forever changing the lives of young people. Aseema's tale demonstrates the enduring impact of persistent commitment to empowering individuals and altering communities.

Dilbur and Aseema's journey over the last 25 years enables us to imagine a world in which education transcends borders, allowing every child to reach their limitless potential. I hope it inspires us to create an equal and inclusive future in which no child is left behind.

– Priyanka Chopra Jonas
Actor

* * *

I have seen the art done by the Aseema children for many years and am delighted that Dilbur has shared what the children learn at the Aseema schools in her book. I have always found their work to be of high quality, with a good understanding of colours, textures, perspective, and forms. This shows that the children are very creative and what I find particularly encouraging is that the Aseema schools expose them to art from all over the world. I do hope that this book will be widely read. It shows us how education can transform lives and motivate all of us to do whatever we can to assist those less fortunate.

– Senaka Senanayake
Contemporary Sri Lankan Artist

* * *

Contents

Foreword

By Adama Dieng, former UN Under-Secretary-General and Special Advisor on the Prevention of Genocide

I first met Dilbur in January 1990. She had just joined the International Commission of Jurists (ICJ), a non-governmental organisation (NGO), headquartered in Geneva, Switzerland, whose primary mission is to advocate for the respect of fundamental rights and freedoms and defend the rule of law around the world. She had been appointed to the position of a legal officer for Asia and the Pacific while I served as the legal officer for Africa. During our initial interactions, my first impression of her was that she was an intelligent and hardworking young attorney who was passionate and exceptionally committed to the cause of human rights and the rule of law. She was keen to make a difference. Our Secretary-General, Niall MacDermot, retired that year in July. Following a lengthy selection process of over 300 candidates from all parts of the World, I became the seventh secretary-general and the first lawyer from the Global South to lead the organisation.

In my new capacity as secretary-general, Dilbur assisted me and together we undertook missions to several countries, including the Philippines, Myanmar, India, Thailand, and Sri Lanka, to advocate and engage authorities on human rights and rule of law-related issues. Not only were some of these missions extremely sensitive and complex, but during this period, human rights and the rule of law were also under serious assault in several countries. Our role was therefore to engage the highest level of national authorities while advocating for the independence of the judiciary and respect for human rights and fundamental freedoms.

I vividly remember one of the issues that was so complex and sensitive during Dilbur's time as the focal point for the Asia-Pacific file—the so-called comfort women, a euphemism for girls and women in occupied countries who were forced into sexual bondage by the Japanese military during the World War II. Not only was the discussion of this issue politically charged, but it also evoked bitter memories on the whole question of wartime violations of human rights and reparations for the victims for the harm done. Thanks to Dilbur's acumen and tireless efforts, ICJ played a major role in ensuring that the victims' stories were put to light and accountability was pursued. Indeed, years on during the 50th anniversary of the end of the war, the Japanese Prime Minister apologised for the harm done and established the 'Asian Women's Fund' which he noted was an expression of atonement on the part of the Japanese people to the victims. This fund was therefore part of efforts to extend the much-needed support for medical, welfare, and other projects on behalf of the victims.

Because of Dilbur's efforts and advocacy, ICJ participated in several missions in the Asia Pacific to advocate for the respect of human rights and the rule of law. For example, we sent trial observer missions to Sri Lanka, East Timor, Indonesia, and Thailand as part of our initiative to promote accountability in the region. We also supported different initiatives in the Asia Pacific especially on the role of paralegals and civil society to provide legal aid and awareness as part of ICJ efforts to promote access to justice and human rights in the region. Other key initiatives included regional seminars that were undertaken in furtherance of the promotion and protection of human rights. For example, the organisation supported seminars on women and law and rights of children in the Asia Pacific. Indeed, the latter seminar was pivotal as it was conducted in the immediate aftermath of the adoption by the United Nations of the Child Rights Convention. It was, therefore, an opportunity to popularise the importance of this crucial treaty to advance the rights of the children in the region.

As I worked with Dilbur and our ICJ colleagues on these initiatives and others, I saw that we shared several values. These included hard work, strong commitment to the rights of the less privileged, empathy for the plight of victims of violations of human rights, general concern for human rights and the rule of law; and the enjoyment of economic and social rights in dignity and freedom. Soon, our careers and lives took different paths. In 2000, after 10 years at the helm of ICJ, I stepped down to pursue other interests. In 2001, I was appointed by the United Nations Secretary-General Kofi Annan, as the UN Assistant Secretary-General and the Registrar of the International Criminal Tribunal for Rwanda. A tribunal was established by the United Nations to address accountability in the aftermath of the worst atrocities committed in Rwanda during the genocide against the Tutsi in 1994. In 2012, I was appointed by the UN Secretary-General Ban Ki-Moon as the UN Under-Secretary-General and Special Adviser on the Prevention of Genocide. During this period, I continued to follow with keen interest the activities and engagements of my former colleagues at the ICJ, long after we had left the organisation.

Meanwhile, Dilbur, as she narrates in this inspiring book, left Switzerland to return to her native India, and in 1995 she co-founded the Aseema Charitable Trust, an NGO whose purpose is to promote and protect the rights of less privileged children and ensure that they are given the opportunity not only to fulfil their potential but also receive high quality and value-based education to become responsible and useful citizens and contribute to a better country and the world. In her own special voice, she tells story after story in the chapters that follow about how Aseema overcame its initial challenges. Under her leadership and vision, the organisation has remarkably grown from a fledgling NGO serving 18 children in its early years to more than 9,000 children by 2023. Meanwhile, its footprints have spread beyond its roots in Mumbai to locations such as Igatpuri, a tribal area near Mumbai, Kanpur, and Lucknow in North India. The organisation's impact is also being felt in other locations; as its mission has become more widely known, supporters have sprung up in places as far-flung as the US, Canada, the U.K., France, Switzerland, the UAE, and many other countries.

As Aseema speeds past its 25th-anniversary milestone, I am humbled and delighted to see that Dilbur and her colleagues have proved to be such faithful stewards of the principles and values we have tirelessly worked together to advance for a better world. I am extremely proud of the fact that Aseema is working tirelessly to provide high-quality education to some of India's poorest and most marginalised children. Aseema is a testimony of what beliefs in a just cause, commitment, and courage can do to achieve the very best in and for humanity. I recommend a copy of this book to everyone. It is my sincere belief that whoever reads this book will understand and appreciate the value and power of an idea and commitment to pursue it in changing and making this world a better place. To quote Mahatma Gandhi: "The greatness of humanity is not in being human, but in being humane." My dear friend Dilbur has just demonstrated that through her efforts to make a better world for the current and future generations. I applaud her and wish her my very best as she pursues this noble objective.

Aseema is a Sanskrit word that means "limitless." It is an apt metaphor for the potential that resides in every child. Long may Aseema, and the children it cares for, continue to soar and positively contribute to a better and just world we all desire.

Adama Dieng, November 2023

Adama Dieng is a former Secretary-General of the International Commission of Jurists, UN Under-Secretary-General and Special Adviser on the Prevention of Genocide and the UN Assistant Secretary-General and Registrar of the United Nations International Tribunal for Rwanda. He is currently the Founder and President of the Panafrican Alliance for Transparency and the Rule of Law—African Renaissance (PATROL).

Introduction

"In the beginning, there was no clear road, nor a destination in sight. There was only a problem that needed a solution."

Over the years, many people have asked me what prompted me to start Aseema. The answer I have repeatedly given is that after working in the field of human rights at the international level, I felt that much of the work I had done only skimmed the surface. I had been the legal officer for Asia and the Pacific at the International Commission of Jurists (ICJ) in Geneva for five years and I often wondered what difference our interventions were making, and whether they helped to change the lives of people at the grassroots for the better. Though I loved and thoroughly enjoyed my work and greatly appreciated the work that was being done by the ICJ and the need for intervention at this level, the question kept coming back to me.

The ICJ was one of the most respected human rights organisations in the world and any report or intervention it made was always taken very seriously by governments and given the attention it deserved. I remember very vividly the pin-drop silence in the room whenever Niall MacDermot, Secretary-General of the ICJ at the time, and my first boss there, made a presentation at the UN Commission on Human Rights or at its Sub-Commission. Everyone, including all government delegations, listened attentively and gave it the greatest importance.

My work at the ICJ was to organise fact-finding missions to countries where there were human rights violations and also to send observers to trials to ensure that these were fairly conducted, following due process of law. Senior lawyers, law professors, and sometimes judges went on these missions and prepared reports which we, from the Geneva office, had to present at various UN meetings. We also sent these reports to the heads of the concerned countries, giving them a fair opportunity to put forward their point of view.

Apart from this, I also worked with legal aid organisations in Asia and the Pacific. Over the years, I had the opportunity to travel to Thailand, Indonesia, the Philippines, Pakistan, Japan, Nepal, Cambodia, Fiji, and India. Working on paralegal training with the local organisations was interesting and rewarding. It showed me the gaps that existed between what was meant to be and what actually was.

After five years in Geneva, I wanted very much to return home. The decision was not easy but one that I knew I had to make—perhaps to find an answer to the question that had been constantly at the back of my mind. What could I do to help bridge the gap between all the wonderfully worded international conventions and the squalor on the ground? When I told my then-boss, Adama Dieng, of my intention to return home, he sat back in his chair and said, "Please reconsider your decision. I want you to think carefully about it before you give me your formal resignation. This is a rewarding job and what will you do in Mumbai?" At that time, I had no idea, I only knew that I needed to return home.

I also spoke to my two dear friends, Snehal Paranjape and Neela Kapadia, who were among the first people in whom I confided. "Don't do it," Neela said when I told her about it when she visited my home in Geneva. "You have such a great job. Why leave a place as beautiful and comfortable as Switzerland?"

Snehal, on the other hand, was quite happy when I called her to talk about the possibility of my returning to India. "Good heavens!" she said, "Are you sure? Welcome to the courts!! It will be good to have you back." I told her that I had no intention of getting back to legal practice. "I would now like to work with people at the grassroots. Working at the ICJ has been a wonderful experience, and participating in the UN Human

Rights Commission meetings has been a great learning experience. But I need to do something that I see as making a difference in people's lives. Also, the past seven years—five in Geneva and two years before that in Thailand have been quite exhausting. I want something simpler, something where I will have a little more time to myself, time for other things." Little did I realise that starting and running Aseema would be anything but simple, and clearly not as much time as I thought I would get for myself.

There is also another reason that prompted me to start Aseema, one that I have not often shared.

Years earlier, upon finishing school, I told my parents that I would like to be a teacher. My mom, a teacher herself, dissuaded me: "Do you know how hard you have to work? And all those book corrections to be done. Besides, what will you earn? Teachers, unfortunately, are so poorly paid." Not having any strong views on the subject, and to please my dad, who loved the idea of my becoming a lawyer, I studied law. My father was delighted. Once I got admission to Government Law College in Mumbai, he happily helped me with my studies.

Unfortunately, just a couple of months later, he passed away. I was 19 years old at the time, and we faced a lot of financial difficulties. My brother and sister did whatever they could to help, but they had just started building their careers and had their own families to support. During the three years I spent in law college, it was not possible to buy even one set of new clothes or anything that was not an absolute necessity. It took some years before we were financially comfortable again.

Going through this difficult time taught me a very important lesson. It perhaps sowed the seeds to do something for the economically disadvantaged. I sincerely believe that unless one goes through some hardship oneself, it is difficult to fully understand and empathise with the pain and hardship of another.

Neela and Snehal played major roles in starting Aseema. The three of us met several times at my home in Bandra and over umpteen cups of chai (for Neela and me) and coffee (for Snehal) and sandwiches (from Candies) we talked about what we wanted to do and what needed to be done. Finally, we decided to set up a public charitable trust, which we called Aseema. Snehal handled all the legal formalities in the setting up of the trust and Aseema formally came into existence on November 4, 1995, which also happens to be Neela's birthday!

Aseema means limitless or without boundaries in Hindi and Sanskrit, and we decided to work with Mumbai's poorest children—the street (homeless) and slum children. After some initial studies and research, we decided to focus on providing high-quality, value-based education to children living in Bandra, a suburb of Mumbai where I live.

Snehal, Neela and I meeting at my home

None of us had any background in social work or teaching, and we were not at all sure of what the outcome would be. One thing we were all very sure about was that Aseema should work at the grassroots level—our intervention should be simple and practical. There was no major plan drawn up, only a great desire to do things well and systematically—and we did this using common sense. Years later, a case study on Aseema published by *Knowledge@Wharton*, the online research journal of the Wharton School of The University of Pennsylvania, says it exactly like it happened: "In the beginning there was no clear road, nor a destination in sight. There was only a problem that needed a solution."

Bandra West, where we started our work, is an area where many famous film stars and well-to-do people live. Bandra also boasts of some of Mumbai's finest restaurants, and designer and jewellery shops. Alongside them live many of Mumbai's poorest people. The women work as domestic help, while many of the men are daily wage earners, working at construction sites or in small roadside shops.

Once we decided to work in this part of the city, we drew up a basic questionnaire, followed by a visit to some of the traffic signals in Bandra where scruffy little children begged. Many of them were with their mothers whom I, and Shalini Date, a young teacher we had employed, interviewed. We asked for simple information about the number of people in the family, the education the parents had, whether they worked and, if so, what work they did. Most importantly, we wanted to know if the parents were sending their children to school and whether they were interested in giving them a good education. Almost all the mothers said that they had never been to school and added that they would not want their children to grow up like them— begging on the streets. One of them suggested that we visit the area where they came from—Bandra Reclamation near Rangsharda Hotel in Bandra West.

Bandra Reclamation at Bandra West, Mumbai

We visited the next day—it was a big pavement community with lots of little children who greeted us cheerfully. The adults viewed us with some suspicion. When we told them why we had come, one of the women said frankly, "You are not the only ones to come here; many others have visited in the past. They have started *balwadis* (pre-primary schools for children aged three to six years), but nothing has continued for long. People work here for about six months and then they go away."

That statement has stayed with me till today. I prayed that I would never let the children or their parents down. Over the years we have faced obstacles and many difficulties—at the hands of government officials, politicians, financial problems, difficult parents, and even colleagues and staff, but I can honestly say that we have done and continue to do whatever is in our power to give the children the best we can.

While we have worked in schools run by the Municipal Corporation of Greater Mumbai (MCGM) for 20 years and have raised the standards in both academics as well as co-curricular activities like arts, sports, and music, the umpteen difficulties we still face at the hands of the bureaucracy has made us often question what we are doing.

In Igatpuri, a small town some 60 miles from Mumbai, where we have set up a school for tribal children, the trials have been many. They range from a court case to prevent a garbage depot from being set up by the local municipal council opposite our school and the villagers' only water source, to government officials issuing notices to shut down the school. Village politics has also got in the way, with troublemakers spreading rumours about us converting the children to other religious faiths. False news about us kidnapping the children has also made the rounds. All this has led to us spending much time in government offices and courts taking away precious time that could have been better spent in the schools, improving educational standards, strengthening the organisation, and putting it on a firmer footing. What has kept us going through all these distractions is our faith and belief in the children and in ourselves. "Keep on, keeping on" has been our motto! Difficult times will come, but we must hold on to the faith and do what we believe is right. With all sincerity, I can say that we have never given in to pressure. To the best of our ability, we have lived up to the expectations of our young students.

A few days after starting Aseema's education centre in 1997, I visited my elder sister, Arnavaz, in Pune. We both follow the teachings of the great Indian yogi, Paramahansa Yogananda, author of one of the most widely read books on yoga, *Autobiography of a Yogi*. For many years, Arnavaz organised meditation sessions in the beautiful bungalow she was staying in at the time. In December 1997, after one of the sessions, I told her what Snehal, Neela, and I planned to do and also about the children who had been coming to our evening centre. "So many children in Mumbai are out of school and do not have access to good quality education. We intend to reach out to the poorest of the poor," I told her as we sat talking in the hall, which was so wonderfully charged with the positive energy of the satsang (meditation session). "We believe it is important to teach the children what is relevant and meaningful, not conventional education with its focus simply on test scores and unhealthy competition," I continued.

"The kind of education envisaged by Paramahansa Yogananda, with its emphasis on values and developing the power of concentration, is what you should pursue," advised my sister. She was someone whose advice I always took seriously and tried to follow. Both she and my elder brother, Sorab, a solicitor, and their families have always been a great emotional support and source of encouragement to me, which has made my work infinitely easier.

Back in Mumbai, I re-read the chapter from *Autobiography of a Yogi* on the school that Paramahansa Yogananda had started in Ranchi. It also contained Yoganandaji's thoughts on education and his 'How to Live' philosophy. They influenced me tremendously. This was the starting point of the kind of education we were trying to impart at Aseema with an emphasis on truth, simplicity, humility, hard work, and love for all humanity. This became the foundation for all our work at Aseema—both for the children and the adults.

SECTION 1

ASEEMA'S BIRTH

01

The Beginning

Year1:18 Children; One Employee; One Centre

"Please stand in a line." This remark meant little to the 18 happy children, each one of whom was on a frolic of their own! After the initial visit to Bandra Reclamation, these 18 children started attending the education centre started by Aseema on December 15, 1997. They were aged three to 12 years and lived at Lalmitti (which literally means red earth), an area at Bandra Reclamation, in homes made of plastic sheets or, if their parents could afford it, tin sheets and a slightly more permanent structure.

The teacher patiently explained what she meant by standing in a line and some of her students joyfully cooperated while the rest continued to do whatever they were busy with. And the yoga class started. It was a chaotic class, with the teacher trying to calmly explain the instructions and demonstrate what she wanted the children to do. However, though eager to perform, many struggled to follow the instructions.

The children who came to the centre had either never been to school, or had dropped out of it. Some of them continued attending local municipal schools and came to the centre only to learn English. Classes were conducted daily at St. Stanislaus High School, a reputed school in Bandra. The principal of the school, Fr. Lawrence Ferrao, fondly called Fr. Lawrie, had very kindly given Aseema the use of a classroom after school hours, and classes were conducted from 4:00 to 6:00 p.m., Monday through Saturday.

Perhaps this gesture was fuelled by the charitable past of the school, considering it started as an orphanage run by Jesuit priests. I have always remembered Father Lawrie as a kind man, with full faith that we could make a difference in the children's lives. With the evening sun pouring over the large football field that overlooked our classroom, Aseema had finally put down its roots.

At first, the attendance of the children was irregular—the little ones would only come if the older children brought them along. The area where they lived was a 20-minute walk from the school through a very crowded market. To ensure better attendance, I asked all the children to assemble outside one of their homes daily so that we could all walk together to the school. The children loved this—they enjoyed walking through the market, chatting about everything they saw along the way!

I enjoyed this as well—rounding up the children every day (as many of them failed to assemble at the appointed place on time—some still getting ready, some combing their hair, others helping to gather the missing ones). I also enjoyed our simple, interesting walk through the market. On one occasion, the entire road had been dug up, which, though difficult to walk on, made it very interesting for the children. "Like the craters on the moon," they all said, this being something they had just learnt at the centre! At times they would walk singing a song they had learnt and curious shopkeepers and residents would enquire where the little group was off to. When I explained, many offered to help and one even threw them a little party.

Aseema, at that time, worked only with the help of volunteers. Funding was limited and the only teacher we could afford left after a couple of months, saying it was all too much for her. The children were naughty and could be quite exhausting, but like all children, they were lovely! Many of them had never entered a classroom before and took great delight in scampering over the big, heavy, old-fashioned desks. They hopped merrily from desk to desk, and most of all, enjoyed playing with the electric switches, turning them on and off and on again! I was always worried that Fr. Lawrie would come in unannounced, see the chaos and pandemonium, and throw us all out—but that never happened. What I did not know, and learnt many years later from Maria D'Souza, a teacher at St. Stanislaus who worked with Aseema after retirement, was that Fr. Lawrie would quietly observe the children coming to school and marvel at their enthusiasm and "the spring in their step".

The children came daily, some of them neat and tidy, others a little scruffy. Repeated reminders to come clean and neatly dressed had little effect on them. Then one day, one of the volunteers suggested we get a mirror to school. This worked like magic! As soon as they entered the classroom, the children would go first to the mirror, take a good look at themselves, and then set about combing their hair, going to the washroom, and coming back well-scrubbed and clean.

The owner of one of the salons near the school offered to cut the children's hair from time to time. They enjoyed this very much, sitting in front of the big mirrors and having one of the beauticians gently handling their hair. It was on one such visit to the salon that little Sanju, aged five years while sitting in front of the mirror, realised that one of his eyes looked different from the other and tried hard to cover the eye with his hand. Sanju had a bad squint and when the teacher saw him doing that, she promised to take him to a doctor. Somewhat pacified, he agreed. A visit to the eye hospital revealed that the defect was very severe and could only be partially rectified. Before any treatment could be undertaken, Sanju's family left Mumbai and went back to their village.

Around this time, major changes were taking place in the world. In the United Kingdom, the Labour Party won its largest election victory in history and Tony Blair became the U.K.'s youngest prime minister at the age of 44. A year later, Bill Clinton was re-elected in the US with a landslide victory. Closer home, the Civil War in Sri Lanka intensified. At home, K.R. Narayanan became the President of India in 1997, becoming the first member of the Dalit community to hold the post.

Sanju and his story wouldn't make an impact on the world like these stories did, but it did impact me. It reminds me, every day, just how much the children's home life affects their education and well-being.

Many of the people who live in the shanties at Bandra Reclamation come from different parts of Maharashtra, and the rest of India. They come mostly from rural India and the reason they come to Mumbai and live in such abysmal conditions is that they have no work in their villages. Many of them own small pockets of land in the village, but water is scarce and they can only cultivate a few crops during the monsoon. There are no irrigation facilities, and for a few months before the monsoon sets in, not even clean drinking water. In 1997, few villages had electricity or toilets, and open defecation was common. While the Government of India has done much work in recent years to provide electricity and build toilets in rural areas, these problems still exist in many places. Medical facilities are of very poor quality, and in many places, totally non-existent.

I was once in a taxi in Mumbai, a city where the traffic is terrible and traffic jams are the norm when I started talking to the taxi driver.

The elderly man looked harassed and tired and mentioned that he was from North India and had lived in Mumbai for over 20 years. When I asked him why he had left his village and come to Mumbai, he replied, *"Mumbai ek shahar hai jo subka pet bharti hai"*. (Mumbai is one place where no one goes hungry).

Three months after the centre started, a lady came up to me in the marketplace and said, "I have been watching the children and you walking through the market every day. Is there anything I can do to help bring them to school?" At first, I wondered why she offered to help—was it because she felt that I was tired, was it due to the goodness of her heart, or was it because she wanted her young children also to come to the centre to be educated? I didn't overthink it, and happily accepted the offer! From that day onwards, Shobha Gaikwad brought the children daily from their homes to the centre, a practice she followed for over 15 years, till she secured a better-paying government job. Shobha was enthusiastic and took great pride in her work and was delighted that her two young children, Ashish and Nirmala would now learn English and go to good schools.

The first few months at the centre were not easy. At times, the children had to be coaxed to come. They had little understanding of time—we would tell them that they had to come to class by a particular time, but that had no meaning in their scheme of things. Three o'clock meant any time between 3:00 to 4:00 p.m. It was a great lesson in patience.

Not much formal learning happened initially. It was more about creating a happy and understanding, caring and secure environment—of letting the children know that it was really important for them to learn, that we had faith in them and believed that education could change their lives. It is a belief we still hold on to firmly—that given the right opportunities, our children can do as well as children from economically privileged backgrounds. They have now proved us right; they have not only done as well, but many have done even better. And given the odds that they face, this is a great achievement.

In June 1998, the day the centre reopened after the summer break, I got a frantic telephone call from Shobha, "Teacher, teacher, please do something, please come quickly; our homes are being demolished." A few volunteers and I were already in the classroom at St. Stanislaus waiting to welcome the children back after the vacation. We rushed to the area where the children lived, a site next to the Rang Sharda Hotel at Bandra Reclamation. As we arrived, we saw bulldozers leaving the area. There was flat land where the children's homes once stood. The plastic sheets and other materials that made up their homes had been pushed into the sea, together with all their belongings, including possessions precious to the children. A small doll, and what had once been a toy car, could be seen crushed under the weight of the bulldozer. It was a rainy day, and we were close to tears seeing the destruction.

Shobha and the other parents of our children who lived in the area explained how quickly the bulldozers had come, not even giving them a chance to retrieve their belongings—cooking pots, clothes, and the few pieces of furniture they possessed. Every belonging had simply been shoved into the sea behind their homes. *"Teacher, mera table bhi nahi nikalne diya"* ("Teacher, they did not even let me retrieve my table."), wailed Shobha. According to the municipal authorities, these were all illegal hutments, but the manner in which the entire exercise had been carried out was inhuman and heartless.

The children, however, were in high spirits and delighted to see their teachers. They explained, very excitedly, what had happened. While it seemed like an adventure to them, it was painful for us to see the little ones pointing to their few simple belongings crushed into the earth and being washed away in the torrential downpour.

This continued to happen for the next few years. Early June, the start of the academic year, and the monsoon brought the dreaded bulldozers to this area until all concerned just accepted it as one more hardship to be endured—wanton destruction, then picking up the pieces, rebuilding homes, and getting on with life.

As word spread about Aseema's work, one evening a well-dressed lady walked into the classroom with a carton of toys for the children. After their studies, a little time was kept for play and the children ran happily to the carton and quickly grabbed whatever they could. Every day, six-year-old Shankar, one of the more energetic boys, collected most of the toys and simply sat clutching them. He did not play with them but made sure no one else could have them either. When it was time to leave, the teacher had a difficult time getting Shankar to put the toys back. Slowly, over the months, Shankar got used to taking only one toy at a time, learnt to enjoy himself with it, and shared the toys with the other children.

We also had a volunteer doctor who visited the centre at regular intervals. The children frequently had colds and coughs, fever, skin irritations, and other minor infections. The doctor advised us to spend our limited financial resources on nutrition instead of medication, as she found many of our children were extremely underweight. So, the children were given a banana every day. It would have been wonderful to give them a full meal, but money was limited and bananas were a good option. Shobha brought bananas daily, and the children enjoyed them very much. Sometimes when the money did not last till the end of the month, biscuits were given, and on rare occasions when money completely ran out, nothing was given. But the children still continued to come.

02

The Centre Grows

A sense of purpose and the enthusiasm and love of the children kept us engaged and together.

Through 1998, our evening classes at St. Stanislaus continued with a skeletal staff and very committed volunteers. Alice Francis, a retired and very experienced teacher, was the mother of my best friend in school, Karen. In April 1998, when she heard about Aseema, she promptly came forward to help and continued as a teacher for many years, till she left for Australia to be near her daughter. She was a wonderful teacher—caring, compassionate, and very dedicated and the children loved her.

The day the centre started, there were only two of us, Shalini Date and me, and over a dozen little children of every age all over the place. Things naturally got very chaotic. I realised we desperately needed help and that evening called Tasneem Doctor who had done her social work training at the prestigious Tata Institute of Social Sciences (TISS) in Mumbai. Tasneem had been recommended by another volunteer, Ayesha Irani, and she immediately stepped in the next day armed with some lovely books. The children took to her really well and settled down, much to everyone's relief! Tasneem continued volunteering at Aseema for many years, often bringing her little daughter tucked under her arm to school, making sure she did not miss class.

The other volunteers who came regularly included Ayesha Irani, Dinaz, Armeen Anklesaria, and their friend Jharna Roy Chaudhury. As word about our work spread, others joined—Chandni D'Silva, Sharmila D'Souza, Nilufer Patel, and many of my nieces and cousins pitched in to help whenever they could—Delnaz Mistry, Anahita DeVitre and her children Arzanne and Zarir, Zarin Devitre, her daughter Dilber and my sister-in-law Tannaz Parakh and niece Zia.

Shobha continued to bring the children to class and Munni Waghmare helped to clean the classroom and keep things neat and tidy. They both accompanied the children to the washroom, which was quite a distance away and made sure the children combed their hair and cut their nails regularly.

The most popular person by far was Bella Albuquerque, who, once we could afford a snack, brought something yummy for the children every alternate day, initially, and then every day. Around 6:00 p.m. after two hours of studying, everyone waited for Bella, who would appear wearing her trademark scarlet lipstick. As she crossed the big football field towards our classroom, Shobha and some of the children would go running to help her with her big basket. Bella was large-hearted and extremely fond of us all. She also supplied the snacks at our staff meetings and training sessions and everyone, children and adults, looked forward to her ribbon sandwiches and coconut cake!

Since many of our volunteers had no teaching background or experience, we regularly organised training sessions on effective learning practices. In the early years, training was conducted at my home, as we had no office. One of the earliest training sessions was by Melanie Pereira, who taught the Early Childhood Care and Education (ECCE) course at Sophia Polytechnic. Melanie was a superb teacher and very creative. We learnt a lot from her and she continued to help us for many years.

Hazel Branche, another senior kindergarten teacher, conducted sessions for our volunteers too. She was in her late 70s but had the energy and spirit of a 17-year-old! Juhi Sarkar, a respected municipal school headmistress and a national award winner, trained us as well in the early years.

Bella bringing the evening snack

Several other people came forward to help, including the students of St. Stanislaus. Maria D'Souza extended her assistance in every possible way when help was needed at the school.

With few resources and with the help of volunteers like Delnaz and Nilufer, the children made beautiful wrapping paper, painted lanterns, printed on cloth bags, and made tie-and-dye serviettes, which we displayed at our stall at Concern India Foundation's 1998 fair at the lovely Cricket Club of India (CCI) grounds.

The years we spent in that little classroom at St. Stanislaus were busy and very happy. There was very little structured teaching. The teachers and volunteers shared a lot of stories, there was much singing and learning through nursery rhymes and poems and art and craft—our focus through it all was on creating good human beings.

Initially, all our educational material was stored in a steel trunk in the classroom. Some months later, Anahita DeVitre, donated an old cupboard to the centre. One leg of the cupboard was broken, so it tilted to one side and we kept it in a corner so that it would not fall on anyone. That cupboard was the first piece of furniture Aseema owned, and we all loved it dearly.

When the state board examinations were conducted in the school, we were not allowed to use the classroom, so we would pile our books and materials into the trunk and trudge with them to a public garden nearby. When this first happened, it bothered us greatly, but eventually, we enjoyed conducting classes in the garden and the children were delighted to be outdoors with their teachers.

There was a sense of togetherness and purpose, and the children's enthusiasm and love kept us all engaged and happy.

SECTION II

ASEEMA'S INFANCY

03

Sri Atmananda Memorial School

*The most valuable gift you can give a child is to let her know she
is valued, and that her thoughts and feelings matter.*

Soon after Snehal, Neela, and I registered Aseema as a charitable trust, we undertook the study of the laws and court judgements that affected children in India. We commissioned two researchers for this project— Asha Bajpai from the Tata Institute of Social Sciences and Sangeeta Kamdar, an economics lecturer at Bombay University. The study revealed that India had both laws and court judgements safeguarding the rights of all children. Why then, we wondered, did we see so many children working in factories, making fireworks, matchsticks, bangles, locks, footballs, carpets, and worse, as bonded agricultural labour? Were children not expected to be in school? Did India not have schools run by municipal corporations and councils in every city and town? And was there not supposed to be a school in every village?

What about Bandra, a so-called elite area—where we lived? Had the children we saw begging at every traffic signal ever been to school? If not, why not?

We decided we would ensure that at least a few children who lived in our neighbourhood, attended school regularly.

The United Nations Convention on the Rights of the Child, 1989, which India has acceded to, affirms the right of the child to quality education. The Supreme Court of India too held that every child in the country had a right to free education until the age of 14, and their right to education thereafter was subject to the limits of economic capacity and development of the state. Why not, in a small way, try to make this a reality?

Snehal, Neela, and I felt very strongly that the gap between pontificating about these rights and the reality needed to be bridged. And so, we set up the education centre for children who, for some reason or another, did not have access to quality education. I was excited; it was something I believed in and really wanted to do. It was our chance to make the Convention on the Rights of the Child come alive! A few nagging doubts remained—with no teaching or social work experience. How should we do it and where do we start?

We had set up an advisory board consisting of reputed professionals and people who were very competent in their respective fields. Justice P.N. Bhagawati, the former Chief Justice of India was one of the members of our advisory board, and also senior lawyers Rafiq Dada and Fredun DeVitre, academics Meenaz Kassam, Aloo Dastur, Usha Thakkar, and Kalindi Muzumdar, film director Saeed Mirza, senior bureaucrat Asoke Basak, and Nawshir Khurody from the corporate world. Feruzi Anjirbag, a communication professional, was also on our advisory board. Feruzi had been a great help in drafting Aseema's objectives and goals in the early years.

It was Neela and Feruzi who suggested I visit a school in Kerala, the Sri Atmananda Memorial School, to learn more. The school was in a small village called Malakkara, a three-hour drive from Kochi. So, I enrolled for a month-long course there.

The school had separate sections and campuses for the pre-primary, the primary, and the secondary, and it was run by the Atma Vidya Educational Foundation. Their approach to education was based on respect for the child and creating a secure and creative environment at the school, which appealed to me tremendously. The bond between the teacher and the child was of paramount importance and I saw all this actually being put into practice.

The principal, Tarla Nanavati, a very gentle and kind lady, and the trustees were followers of a spiritual head who lived in the village.

Many of them and some of the teachers were from the United States of America and different parts of Europe. The local teachers and other staff lived in the villages around the school and though many were not followers, they had imbibed this approach. While a great deal of freedom was given to the child in deciding what he was going to study at school, it was the teachers' and volunteers' job to ensure that the child was learning what was relevant and meaningful.

Most of the children arrived on the school bus, having been picked up from the villages in the area. Every morning, the teachers and volunteers would stand at the entrance of the school to welcome them. A "good morning" or "hello", or even a caring touch or eye contact, made every child feel special. Every child was made to feel welcome, even the naughtiest little ones!

Assembly in the pre-primary school was simply the lighting of a lamp with the teachers and volunteers standing around singing a bhajan (hymn), and children who wanted to, joined in. The others did whatever they pleased—some sat and observed the teachers, some participated in the reverence and others raced around, making quite a commotion. The teachers continued calmly singing the beautiful hymn.

In the pre-primary and primary, there were different rooms—a science room, a maths room, a library, an art room, and so on, and the children were free to choose where they wanted to go. The teacher in that class was expected to ensure that the child learnt something in the few minutes or perhaps hours he or she spent in that room. No one said "no" to any child. A more creative way had to be found by every teacher to make sure that the child learned and imbibed some positive behaviour.

There was a little boy who was in a very destructive mood one day. He was playing with aeroplanes and made sure they crashed into all the buildings in the game, killing all the 'people' and creating havoc all around. As he was absorbed in this violent behaviour, one of the volunteers who had been observing him asked if, after all the destruction, he would like to build and create something anew. He quietly looked at her and nodded and just like that, the game changed to one where new buildings were built and the sick were taken care of in a new hospital that had also been built. The volunteer quietly showed how negative behaviour can be changed to positive behaviour in a very subtle way.

At the end of every day, after the children had left, the teachers and volunteers would discuss the events of the day—things that had gone well and things that hadn't. Teachers would discuss cases they had found difficult to handle, and some of the senior teachers or at times even the younger teachers would offer advice. It was a time to share and think things through together. Teachers were also encouraged to write their observations and comments in notebooks that were maintained for every child.

A huge tree crashed down on the playground

One day, after a destructive storm, a huge tree came crashing down on the playground. There was much excitement, and the whole school spent the entire day around the enormous tree. There was a great deal to learn from the tree and tremendous fun learning! Regular schoolwork was set aside for the day, but it did not matter as the learning continued, with many questions asked and answered. The tree was explored to the fullest, and that was all that was important.

By the time the children reach primary school, they want to pray the hymn along with their teachers—no one forces them to do so or tells them they must! This encourages a feeling of devotion, which is seen so rarely at most school assemblies.

By secondary school, the children grow to love their studies, which are much more structured. They learn well and the results are good. In the lower primary section, they are free to decide which activities to attend and how to organise their day. In the upper primary section, children are motivated towards group projects that require a longer attention span. At this time, examinations are introduced in a fun way through an 'Exam Fest' where everyone can help each other. By high school and higher secondary, the children prepare for the external board examinations like any other school.

When I finished the training programme and left Kerala, I knew that much of what I had seen and learnt needed to be put into practice, both by me and all those working at Aseema. Above all, the care, concern, patience, and compassion shown by the teachers at the Atmananda Memorial School were very special. I realised that it was even more important in our case as our children came from homes that had so little to offer. The parents were so focused on earning and living for the day that the children were rarely given a chance to express themselves. They were seldom heard. Also, the focus of the Atmananda School to develop a bond between the teacher and child was crucial. The most valuable gift you can give a child is to show them they are valued, and that their thoughts and feelings matter. How to put all this into practice in Mumbai was another matter—I only knew and believed that it had to be done.

04

Our Montessori Centre

The child is at the centre of learning and the teacher has to simply follow the child and become aware of the true nature of the child.

Very soon we realised that the children were capable of doing well if they were given the right opportunities. So, in April 1998, at a parent-teacher meeting at the centre, we told the parents that from June of that year, it would be advisable to have their children admitted to mainstream schools as well. The parents initially resisted, saying that they would not be able to pay the school fees. "Don't worry," we confidently told them. "We will cover the fees. Your part is to ensure that the children attend school regularly, every single day, and on time." Where that confidence came from is as much a mystery today as it was then! Perhaps it stemmed from a belief that the Divine would support any worthwhile cause!

The following June, we had most of the children who attended the centre admitted to formal schools, some to private schools in the area, and many to local municipal schools.

Soon we encountered two problems—one, the older children aged seven to 12 years had had no firm educational foundation and found it very difficult to cope with their studies. The second problem was that the children who had been admitted to the municipal schools began to forget all that they had learnt earlier, as the quality of the education they received for a host of reasons was not very good.

At the time, we were very fortunate to have a volunteer, Nicola Dadyburjor, who had completed the Montessori course conducted by Zarin Malva of the prestigious Association Montessori International

(AMI). Nicola made it very clear on her first day at Aseema that she had "just come to see" what Aseema was doing and how we worked. She saw and stayed, overseeing the education programme, and later became a trustee at Aseema.

Nicola taught at a private Montessori school in the morning and came to Aseema in the afternoon, as our classes were conducted from 4:00 to 6:00 p.m. every evening. Bina Parekh, who ran the private Montessori school, where Nicola worked every morning, was a lovely person, well-intentioned, and generous. She was eager, after her morning school got over, to let Aseema use her school to run a Montessori class for our children. Nicola worked with the youngest age group at our centre every evening—children aged two-and-a-half to four years—and she found their progress rather slow.

"Sitting in one place on desks and chairs doesn't appeal to them," she said. "Little children like and need to move around, explore things around them, it helps their all-round development." She gave me a few books written by Dr Maria Montessori[1] and invited me to Harmony, Bina's new Montessori school, where she worked. The visit to Harmony was my first visit to a Montessori school for children aged two-and-a-half to six. It was lovely, with everything child-sized, child-friendly, and aesthetically designed—truly a happy children's house!

We immediately accepted Bina's generous offer and Nicola and I made plans to start our evening classes there from the following academic year, June 2000. Just before we started discussing this matter with our

---

1   *Maria Montessori was a doctor, lecturer, and researcher in Italy and a well-educated woman of her time. She experimented with the education of children and the methods, materials, and system she devised were so successful that today some of the best pre-primary schools all over the world (about 15,000) follow the Montessori approach. She believed that given the right environment, a child will show their true nature and that the purpose of education is to equip a person to deal with all of life; to create a harmonious and peaceful society, and to consider ourselves belonging to one human family responsible for maintaining our earthly home.*

children's parents, Bina dropped a bombshell—it would not be possible for us to use her school. The reason is that some of the parents of the children who came to Harmony may object to our scruffy and naughty youngsters coming to the same school and using the same material. We were extremely disappointed but realised that Bina had really and truly gone out of her way to help but was, in fact, as helpless as we were to address this unhappy situation.

After lengthy discussions with Nicola, we decided to set up our own Montessori centre. We were enthusiastic and very ambitious and determined to make it the very best Montessori in Mumbai!

Thus, the first Montessori centre in India for underprivileged children was set up in a room at the Pali Chimbai Municipal School in Bandra in August 2000. In this room, a class was taken by Poonam Vajandar, a gentle and caring teacher, for our older children following a more conventional curriculum in the morning, and was converted into a Montessori for our two-and-a-half to six-year-olds in the afternoon. Nicola and Geeta Gala, both wonderful Montessori teachers, lovingly and painstakingly created a perfect Montessori environment. They prepared beautiful teaching aids in many creative ways and we ordered the Montessori apparatus from Kaybee in Hyderabad, at the time perhaps the only manufacturer of such apparatus in India. When the first lot of material arrived, there was great excitement! You can imagine the children's (and our) delight when the beautiful material was displayed on low, open shelves.

First came the exercises of practical life (EPL) material. EPL helps children develop care for themselves, their environment, and one another. These activities also build a child's concentration and nurture their motor skills. They include simple activities like rolling and unrolling a mat, lifting and putting down a chair, opening and closing boxes and other objects, folding napkins, pouring and offering a glass of water or tea, sweeping and dusting objects, mopping the floor, washing clothes, arranging flowers, etc.

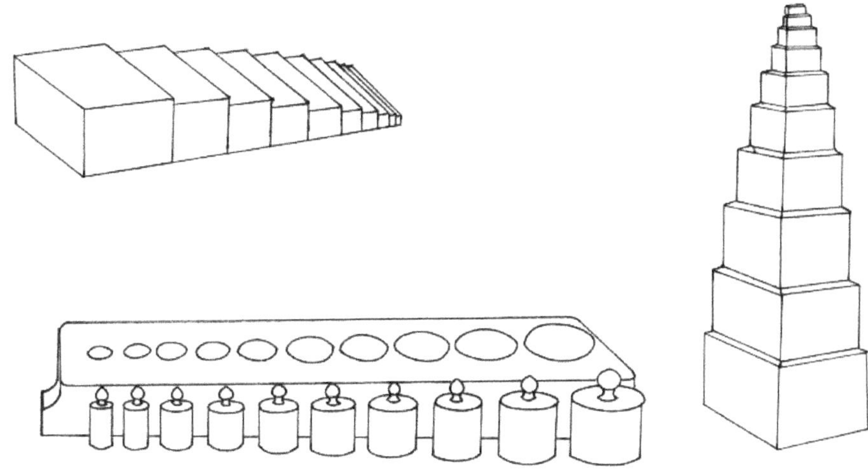

Montessori apparatus

Then came the sensorial materials, which help children develop their senses and explore their environment in a meaningful way. These include coloured boxes, cylinder blocks, a pink tower, long stairs, geometrical cabinets and cards, construction triangles, and binomial and trinomial cubes. Then came the coloured cylinders, metal insets, botany cabinet, touch boards, a box of fabrics, sound boxes, and other materials. Number rods, spindle boxes, and golden bead material adorned the maths shelves, while much of the language material was prepared by the teachers.

Every afternoon, the older students would leave the room after their class and Nicola and Geeta would remove the Montessori apparatus from the cupboard where it was safely stored. The older children in the Montessori class soon started helping their teachers set up the environment every day and then put it all away at the end of the day. The children realised that something so precious had to be treated with great love, care, and respect—and this was the first important lesson that they learned.

In June 2002, we started one more Montessori class in the morning and were able to accommodate many more children. The older children would attend both batches, morning and afternoon, as they were being prepared to attend the first grade in a mainstream school the following year.

What attracted us to the Montessori philosophy was that the child was at the centre of learning and the teacher had to simply follow the child. If the teacher keenly observes the child, she will see what they need and then accordingly guide them. This makes the teacher aware of the true nature of the child.

Most schools in India, even today, have teacher-centric classrooms that use rote learning and drill. Academic subject matter is not integrated with practical activities and is highly compartmentalised. Many schools simply reward memorisation and are highly competitive, with very little focus on character building.

At Aseema, we wanted the child to enjoy coming to school and to learn what was relevant and meaningful. We believe in laying emphasis on and developing the child's power of concentration, which is at the heart of the Montessori approach. We also believe that rewards and punishment make no difference to a child; that work itself is the reward. We also realised the importance of social grace and courtesy and saw how small children take to this very naturally if they see it being done by the adults, and make it a part of themselves.

And that is why and how our first Montessori centre started.

05

First and Subsequent Visits to Pondicherry

"Pedagogy can, at best, create students of science, students of literature, great critics and commentators but it is facilitation and true learning alone that create the scientist, the poet, the artist, the thinker and the philosopher."

– Partho

I first visited Pondicherry in the year 2007. It was to attend the teachers' camp organised by Sri Aurobindo Society[2] in May—the hottest and most humid month in Pondicherry. Together with a group of five young teachers from another school, I took a flight from Mumbai to Chennai and then a very enjoyable ride by taxi to Pondicherry, now officially called Puducherry and affectionately 'Pondy' by those who love the city. As we entered the town, it was not quite what I imagined it to be. I thought it would be much quieter and quainter with French cafes dotting the streets. Instead, we were driven down busy streets, full of people and chaotic traffic much like you see in any Indian city.

---

2   *Sri Aurobindo was an Indian philosopher, spiritual reformer, and poet. He developed a spiritual practice called 'Integral Yoga'. Mirra Alfassa, reverently called 'The Mother' by her followers, was a collaborator of Sri Aurobindo. They founded the Sri Aurobindo Ashram in Pondicherry in 1926. In 1943, she started a school in the ashram called Sri Aurobindo International Centre of Education (SAICE).*

This Centre provides education from kindergarten to college. Its facilities include humanities, sciences, languages, engineering, and physical education. Students also learn art, craft, music, dance (both Indian and Western), and dramatics, and there are also opportunities for practical and manual work.

In 1968, The Mother established the universal town of Auroville where people from all around the world could live in peace and harmony, above all politics and nationalities.

And finally, around four o'clock we reached the beautiful Sea Side Guest House which was to be my home for the next two weeks. On entering, I immediately felt peaceful and comfortable. As the name suggests, it had a wonderful view of the sea, which added to its charm.

Teachers and I at the Sea Side Guest House

That evening, I took a short stroll around my guest house. The Sri Aurobindo Society, where the teachers' camp was to be conducted, was only one building away. I entered the beautifully maintained garden of Sri Aurobindo Society which led to the ground-floor hall where Shivakumar, dressed in his trademark white kurta pyjama, was talking to a group of teachers who had arrived for the camp. Our Mumbai group introduced ourselves.

"Welcome to Pondicherry!" said Shivakumar, who we learnt was the coordinator for the camp. "Now you can go and get some rest but please remember to be on time tomorrow," he told us after a brief introduction of what was expected over the next few days. It was a timely reminder of things to come. Discipline, punctuality, and order were still things to be learnt by us who came from chaotic Mumbai!

The camp started the following day. The introduction by Vijaybhai, a trustee of the Sri Aurobindo Society, had me enthralled. He spoke of education in a manner I had never heard before. The entire week was very busy and full of promise, with very interesting sessions by amazing people—resource persons and teachers from both the Sri Aurobindo Society and the Sri Aurobindo International Centre for Education (SAICE). We were introduced to the principles and thoughts of Sri Aurobindo and The Mother on integral education. Shivakumar himself took many of the sessions, which were lucid and very interesting.

We had been asked to read the book on integral education before we attended the camp. The first principle of integral education that 'nothing can be taught' was confusing. What on earth did they mean? What then had all our teachers been doing over the years? When I heard what all these amazing people were revealing to us, I got a glimpse of what real education was. They were not only extremely creative and articulate but more importantly, they practised what they preached, and it was this that made the camp a unique experience. It was as if all my questions were being answered, one by one, and it was what I had been looking for all along, the true essence of education.

The visit to the SAICE, the school started by The Mother, strengthened the belief that it was possible to put into practice all that we had learned. We were taken to the kindergarten where the little ones aged three to six were taught in French and also introduced to Sanskrit. The Flower House, a lower primary school for students from Grades I to IV, was housed in another building. The older students studied at the beautiful school situated opposite the samadhi, the main centre of the ashram. And finally, there was the college, 'Knowledge' for students aged 18 to 21, from which they eventually graduated. At all the different centres, you could see students working in small groups with their teachers, the average student-teacher ratio being 5:1.

Physical education (what we call sports in our schools), for all the students, from kindergarten to those at 'Knowledge' was given great importance and was compulsory on all days of the week, including Sundays. While there was a certain amount of flexibility in the academic section of the school, strict discipline was maintained in the physical education department. It was a familiar sight to see the students walking down the streets of Pondy on their way to the very well-equipped playground and sports ground dressed in the special sports uniform designed for them by The Mother—both girls and boys in white shirts and grey shorts and a special headgear, a 'kitty-cap' for the girls.

Above all, being in the ashram area and visiting the samadhi daily was a very calming and uplifting experience. 'Knowledge' was right next to my guesthouse and every morning, I would hear the beautiful music being played to herald the start of classes. The entire ashram area, with its lovely grey and blue buildings, clean streets, flowering laburnum trees, and the wonderful promenade by the sea had a very special aura, and I knew that our teachers at Aseema would benefit greatly from visiting the place and undergoing such a camp.

I also thought it would be a good idea to expose the Municipal Corporation of Greater Mumbai (MCGM) officials in the education department to what was taking place here. I spoke about it to Vijaybhai who was always very cooperative and he responded very positively, "The message of integral education must spread and we would be very happy to share our thoughts and philosophy with all true seekers."

A few months later, I returned to Pondy with Carolyn Fernandes, the then-education coordinator at Aseema, and Mr Bagnekar, from the MCGM's education department. Both Carolyn and I were members of a committee the High Court had appointed to look into education in MCGM schools, and we desperately wanted things to improve in all their schools. We felt that the positive energy of Pondy, together with the inspiring experiments in education being carried out there, and meeting some of the committed teachers, would surely strike a chord in the MCGM officer's heart. We were hoping that he would want to replicate at least some of what he had seen and learned at the SAICE.

But sadly, none of this led to any change in the MCGM schools. It remained an interesting and pleasant trip, nothing more.

Carolyn, however, was very keen on the Aseema teachers being exposed to all this and so in October 2007, we organised a special training camp for all the Aseema teachers in Pondy. It was fascinating and a real learning for them, both the camp itself and the experience of the ashram area. They came back to Mumbai uplifted and were keen to implement what they had learnt at the weeklong camp.

This training reinforced our belief in the strong bond that needs to be established between teacher and child. It also created a shift in our thinking, from "teaching" to "learning". Further, it encouraged us to give more importance and emphasis to physical education. Finally, and most importantly, it emphasised the tremendous importance of value-based education and the principles of truth, happiness, humility, compassion, gratitude, responsibility, and giving. These were the same how-to-live principles of Paramahansa Yogananda, which is what we had wanted for Aseema at the time of inception. Things were finally coming together and falling into place.

Every subsequent visit to Pondy, and there have been many, has strengthened my belief that education needs to be seen differently. While pedagogy is important, learning happens more through nurturing relationships. As poignantly stated in the book, *Integral Education—A Foundation for the Future*, by Partho, "Pedagogy can, at best, create students of science, students of literature, great critics and commentators but it is facilitation and true learning alone that create the scientist, the poet, the artist, the thinker, and the philosopher."

SECTION III

ASEEMA GROWS IN MUMBAI

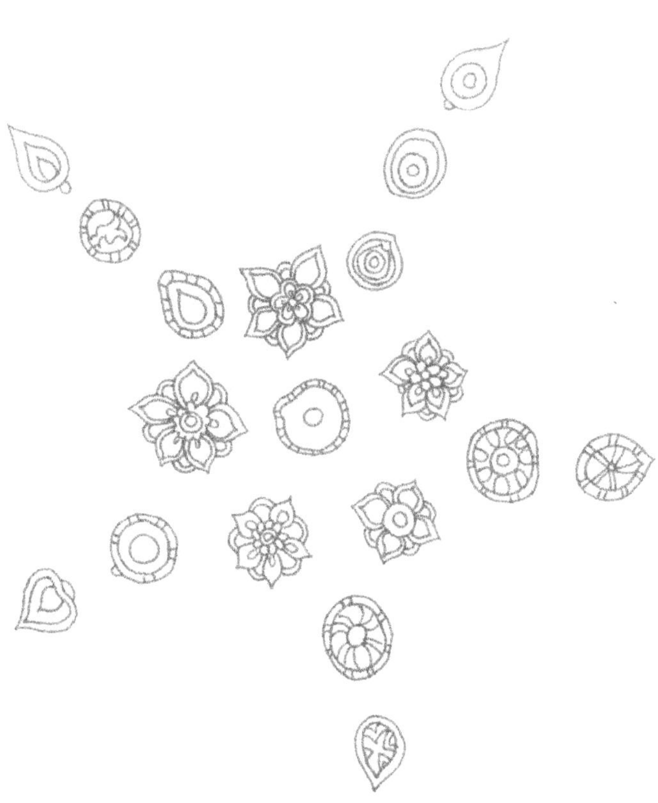

06

Adoption of a Municipal School

A hope and a dream.

Another problem that we encountered was more than we could handle. It involved that big, humongous body called the Municipal Corporation of Greater Mumbai (MCGM). The MCGM ran schools in eight different languages—Marathi, Hindi, Gujarati, Urdu, Telugu, Tamil, Kannada, and English, and though the demand for English-medium schools was high, they were not running very efficiently. The school in which we were running our Montessori centre, the Pali Chimbai Municipal School (PCMS) in Bandra, had seven standards, only one headmistress, and one teacher. The headmistress took classes for three grades and also did all the administrative work of the school. The other teacher taught the other four grades. While the school records showed about 100 children enrolled, the daily attendance was about 40.

In June 2001, the older children from our Montessori class were admitted to PCMS in Grade I. They attended class in the mornings there, and after school, came to our Montessori, which ran from 2:00 p.m. to 4:00 p.m. Nicola and Geeta, the two Montessori teachers, found that the children who had been learning well with them all this time, showed less interest in their studies and forgot what they had learnt earlier. We were flummoxed—what do we do now?

At the time, there appeared an article in *The Times of India*, a leading daily newspaper, that the MCGM was open to offering schools to private parties to "adopt". We immediately wrote to the MCGM, expressing our interest in "adopting" the PCMS. Soon, an officer visited us and gave us an application to fill out, which we did. After a couple of months, the same officer told us that our application had been accepted and handed us a small green booklet that mentioned all the dos and don'ts of adoption. On reading the booklet, we realised that "adoption" meant the donation of desks, chairs, fans, painting of the building, and so on and so forth. Curiously, there was no mention of what could be done to improve the quality of education!

Aseema had few resources at the time, but above all, we wanted to make sure that the children were learning well. We, therefore, appointed a teacher, Masarrat Vasi, and placed her in Grade 1 at the school. We also thought that the MCGM headmistress would be delighted to have some extra help, but we were sorely mistaken. Our assistance was unfortunately looked upon as interference and things were quite difficult for Masarrat, who was enthusiastic and committed and tried to give the children her very best.

While the school had a lovely location, the building had not been maintained well. The drainage system was in shambles and the toilets, the less said about them, the better. We did not have the necessary resources to improve the infrastructure at the school, though we desperately needed a better environment. Which teacher would stay on in the school if she could not even go to the toilet, we wondered? We were truly blessed to have those that did, such was their commitment. As for the children, what was ironic was that they continued to have lessons on cleanliness and hygiene when, in fact, everything in their immediate school environment—from toilets to classrooms to playground, was in a state of disrepair.

The Pali Chimbai Municipal School before renovation

Aseema had started receiving a few donations and we were able to afford a couple of teachers and cover other incidental expenses. We also had several volunteers who helped the teachers. However, with our limited resources, it was not possible to carry out any repairs or infrastructure work at the school, so we continued to work under difficult conditions and hoped that the municipal corporation would undertake the necessary maintenance and repairs.

The children started taking more interest in their studies thanks to the committed teachers. We had great plans in mind—setting up a nice library, a play area in the compound and overall, a safe, bright, and cheerful environment. But at that stage, it was only a hope and a dream.

07

The Municipal Corporation of Greater Mumbai and the Public-Private Partnership

"But it has always been done this way and no change is possible."

In our first year, after we adopted the Pali Chimbai Municipal School (PCMS), Aseema had one teacher in Grade 1. The following year we added another teacher in Grade 2 and continued to add a teacher every year until 2007, when we had teachers in all classes, from Grades 1 to 7. At the time the PCMS was an upper primary school, which meant that the school only had Grades 1 to 7. For their secondary schooling, children had to enrol elsewhere.

The headmistress, who was appointed by the MCGM, had a love-hate relationship with us. She and other teachers of municipal schools have to perform many administrative duties and also frequently visit the education department and ward offices. This results in their being out of school for the greater part of the day, which adversely impacts the education programme. We did everything possible to cooperate with her on all matters. For us, the most important thing was to not compromise on the quality of education being provided at the school and to make it a happy, caring, and secure environment that the children looked forward to.

With all the hard work put in by the Aseema teachers and staff and improvement in the quality of education, many more children enrolled. In 2001, we had about 100 students on the rolls, but only about 40 attended school. By 2007, the school was running to full capacity.

No child could be refused admission to a municipal school and as more and more children started seeking admission, we approached the headmistress and asked her to limit the number of children per class. I tried to reason with her, "Please, now that the school is doing well, let us ensure that quality is maintained—one teacher cannot handle a class with more than 40 students." She would reply, "My hands are tied. In MCGM schools, we cannot do this. We have to enrol all those who seek admission."

One year, we had to admit all the children who came for admission and there were more than 90 students in Grade 1. It was incredibly difficult for the teacher, but there was no option. It is very difficult to reason with people who simply tell you, "But it has always been done this way and no change is possible."

The Pali Chimbai Municipal School after renovation

To ensure that the children learned well, we formed smaller groups of students and had volunteers sitting in the large corridors of the school with each group. The headmistress and some of the MCGM officers who visited the school would object to this and insist that all children be made to sit in the overcrowded classes. "This is not right," they would tell us, "Make everyone sit inside." So, the children would reluctantly trudge into the overcrowded classroom once again.

At the time, some classrooms were used to store old and broken furniture. Other classrooms were being used by some non-government organisations (NGOs) that did absolutely no work with the children of this school. It was a long and painful struggle to get more classrooms. Only many, many years later and after numerous letters and visits to various MCGM officials were all the rooms finally used as classrooms or for co-curricular activities.

In 2008, when we could no longer cope with the large numbers, we were permitted to run the school in shifts—a morning shift and an afternoon shift, each of five and a half hours. This was a relief to both teachers and students, as the improved student-teacher ratio allowed us to pay more personalised attention to each child. It also meant hiring more teachers, which meant more funding was required, but it was well worth it. The only drawback was that the actual learning time was less than what it was in most schools in Mumbai, which was seven hours.

In Mumbai, the number of children in a class can be anywhere from 15 in an international school, to more than 60, and sometimes even 80 in government and private schools! As can be imagined, the large numbers severely compromise the quality of education. In many schools in India, even children in senior classes are unable to read simple words or sentences or do basic maths.

The 2022 Annual Status of Education Report (ASER)[3] for rural India carried out across 19,060 villages shows that enrolment levels for

---

3   *The Annual Status of Education Report (ASER) is a nationwide rural household survey that reaches every rural district in India. In each sampled village, a government school is also visited. The ASER survey was carried out every year from 2005 to 2014 and then in 2016, 2018, and 2022.*

children aged six to 14 have been high for a decade and reached 98.4% in 2022. Figures for children's attendance is about 72%.

However, as far as learning goes, the picture is still dismal. From 2014 to 2018, there has been a gradual improvement in both basic reading and maths. This was interrupted by the pandemic years.

In 2022, only 25% of all children in Grade 3 were at 'grade level' in maths and 20% in reading. In Grade 5, only 38.5% of children in government schools could read at the Grade 2 level and 21.6% could divide. Only one out of four children in Grade 5 and half the children in Grade 8 could read simple sentences in English, and this has remained constant between 2016 and 2022. Out of those who can read, only 62.3% can comprehend what they read.

Only 44% of schools had library books available and being used while only 7.9% of schools had computers, which were being used by children. Only 68.9% of schools had a playground, up slightly from 66.5% in 2018.

The report concluded that big changes in practice activities and much effort will be needed if all children are to achieve basic foundational literacy and numeracy.

In 2004, I was asked to be part of a committee that the Bombay High Court had appointed to look into the working of all MCGM Schools in Mumbai. A few years earlier, in 1998, an unfortunate incident took place at a municipal school, resulting in the accidental death of a seven-year-old student. Her father filed a writ petition against the MCGM, and while disposing of the petition, the High Court highlighted the deplorable condition of MCGM schools. It appointed a committee headed by a retired judge of the Bombay High Court, Justice D. R. Dhanuka. The Dhanuka Committee visited 51 MCGM schools, all in appalling condition. One school was so dilapidated that the committee declared that "only a miracle held the structure together."

The Dhanuka Committee finally submitted a detailed report with its recommendations. Two years later, the then Acting Chief Justice of the Bombay High Court, Justice A.P. Shah, investigated whether the Dhanuka Committee's recommendations had been implemented. Justice Shah appointed two other committees—one to look into the infrastructure of the schools and the other to look into the quality of education being imparted.

I was asked to be on both committees; at first, I was most reluctant. There was so much to do at Aseema that I didn't want to take on any more work than I could handle. Also, many committees tend to be very bureaucratic. Much time, money, and energy are spent on them and there is ultimately little impact and almost no change at the grassroots level. I discussed this matter with some of my colleagues and they said, "Being on the committee will allow you to visit many other MCGM schools and understand the functioning of the MCGM Education Department much better." There was merit in what they said, and so I agreed.

The other members of the Infrastructure Committee were Dr Alka Karande, the then Deputy Municipal Commissioner (Education) who was the chairperson; Shyam Divan, a leading lawyer at the Bombay High Court; and Rahul Kadri, a well-known architect. The Education Committee consisted of Dr Alka Karande, who also chaired this committee; Zarine D'Monte, a leading child psychotherapist; Carolyn Fernandes, who had considerable teaching experience; and Asha Bajpai from the Tata Institute of Social Sciences (TISS).

Over the years, there were many, many meetings and also many visits to schools. It was on such visits that I realised that Justice Dhanuka was absolutely right in stating, "Only a miracle held the structure together!" Considering no further mishaps have taken place, it certainly seems what a dear friend once pointed out: "God definitely lives in India"!

Finally, a system was put into place by the Infrastructure Committee for major school repairs and a dedicated infrastructure cell exclusively for MCGM schools came into being. For the first time, architects were to work in collaboration with contractors, and consultants were appointed to oversee their work. Repairs and renovations of all MCGM schools were to be carried out as per the manuals prepared by the Infrastructure Committee. Some good, creative architectural firms undertook the work of school infrastructure repairs and we were pleased that after several years, we were finally seeing positive results in some of the schools. However, the MCGM had made things so difficult for some of the architects that they were reluctant to undertake any further projects. As one of the architects said to us, "There is simply no coordination or agreement between the education department of the MCGM, which is the user, and the engineering department, which undertakes the school repairs. They make it impossible to work and this is the last MCGM school that I will be doing."

A well-constructed and properly maintained school makes a great difference to a child's outlook—a fact to which, unfortunately, little or no attention is paid.

As far as the Education Committee was concerned, I think our biggest contribution was the proposal to have an effective public-private partnership policy. A draft was prepared and, in 2008, the High Court directed the MCGM to implement the revised school adoption and partnership programme.

This was achieved years later thanks to the intervention of a sensitive and intelligent Additional Municipal Commissioner, Ashish Kumar Singh, who truly believed that all children in municipal schools should have access to high-quality education. A committee set up by him in 2010 headed by Mrs Kumud Bansal, Former Secretary for Education, Government of Maharashtra and Former Secretary, Ministry of Human Resource Development, Government of India, finally drafted such a policy, which was approved by the Education Committee, the Standing Committee, and finally the full house of the MCGM in 2013.

As a member of the committee set up by Ashish Kumar Singh, I truly believe that the policy will go a long way in improving the quality of education for Mumbai's most vulnerable children. There is, of course, the possibility of the policy being misused but many of us at Aseema are of the opinion, after having worked in MCGM schools for over 20 years, that even if a few schools are taken up by honest, competent, and credible organisations that have no other agenda but to provide the very best education to the children, the entire exercise will have been well worth it.

The new policy would enable organisations to have complete academic and operational freedom to run the school for 10 years. While the state curriculum will have to be followed, the organisations will be free to choose the pedagogy. Assessments will be carried out by an independent third party, and based on the outcome of the assessments, the organisation will be allowed to continue working in the school.

Unfortunately, in 2018, there was a move to dilute this policy and replace it with a couple of other initiatives. At the time of writing this, Aseema has signed a memorandum of understanding with the MCGM and is awaiting its finalisation. This has taken 10 years since the approval of the policy in 2013 and we are still waiting!

Running an MCGM school is a challenging task—the MCGM provides 27 articles like school uniforms, bags, books, etc. to the students. The building, electricity, and water costs are borne by the MCGM. However, no financial assistance is given for salaries to teachers and other staff, which is a major expense in a school. At times, MCGM officers and MCGM headmasters or headmistresses interfere needlessly in the running of the school. At times, additional classrooms are not provided on time when required, and the amount of paperwork demanded from the teachers is immense.

But all said and done, when we see the happy faces of the children in school; when we see how positively they respond to their teachers; when we see them do well in the board exams, sports, music, dance, and art, we feel it is worth all the difficulties we face. And the biggest joy is when they come back to school when they are in college or working and say, "Teacher, I really want to help, just tell me what I can do."

08

One More Municipal School

Until now, 12 batches of students from Aseema have completed their Secondary School Certificate (SSC) Board Examination with an average pass percentage of 98 %.

Despite the interference by the headmistress and other MCGM officials, our experience of running the Pali Chimbai Municipal School was, by and large, positive. The children were doing well and responding to the shift we made from traditional rote learning to learning more creatively. We were now ready and looked forward to taking on another municipal school in 2007.

It happened when the then Deputy Municipal Commissioner, Mr S.S. Shinde, encouraged non-government organisations such as ours to do more work in municipal schools and targeted setting up 84 new English-medium Mumbai Public Schools (MPS Schools) in the city. Aseema took on one more school under this programme—a secondary school at Santacruz (West)—Gazdar Park Maneckji Municipal Secondary School (SMS). We started a kindergarten section there in 2007 and, a year later, a secondary section. The first floor of the school building was given to us for this purpose.

At the time, there were only 49 secondary schools in Mumbai and 1,200 primary schools. Out of the 49, only one was an English-medium school. Students of municipal schools who had finished their primary education found it very difficult to get admission to a secondary school. Many poor people today prefer not to send their children to MCGM schools, as they have little faith in the quality of education they provide. They save or even borrow money to send them to so-called 'private schools' which they believe are much better. Hence, children who come to MCGM schools are the poorest of the poor in Mumbai.

When these students completed their primary education, they found it impossible to get admission to other schools, and this resulted in many of them dropping out of school altogether. Hence, in 2008, Aseema asked for permission to start a secondary section at the Santacruz school, which was immediately granted. Once we took on this school, we took steps to improve the infrastructure. There were drug addicts living in one of the rooms on the ground floor and it was only after we complained to the then Police Commissioner of Mumbai, Rakesh Maria that they were removed from the school premises.

Until now, 12 batches of students from Aseema have completed their SSC board examination with an average pass percentage of 98%.

In 2009, a person approached Ashok Pawar, our social worker at PCMS, and asked for admission for two children—Rubina Ali Qureshi and Azharuddin Ismail. "They have acted in a movie and the director and producer are keen to have the children get a good education. We would like them to be admitted to your school," she said. After collecting the relevant documents, both children were given admission.

A few months later, leading television and news agencies thronged the school gate, and we had a difficult time keeping them from entering the school. The movie the two children had acted in was *Slumdog Millionaire*, which won eight Academy Awards at the 2009 Oscars, including the Award for Best Film and Director—and the children became little stars overnight!

They went to Los Angeles to attend the Oscar Award ceremony, and once they were back, the media hounded them. We had a difficult time ensuring that they attended school regularly. On one occasion when Rubina's attendance was found to be very poor and her teacher complained, I was asked to intervene. On discussing it with Rubina's father, he said *"Kya kare teacher, Rubina ko Paris me modelling assignment mila tha, isliye school nahin aa saki."* (What can I do teacher, Rubina got a modelling assignment in Paris and hence could not attend school.) Well, what could I say? While I gave him a little lecture on why it was important for her to attend school regularly, I realised that acting and modelling had taken precedence over school studies and assignments. Fortunately, she was a very intelligent girl and managed to catch up with the rest of the class despite her frequent absence from school. In her final year at the PCMS, she was elected head girl. She chose not to secure admission to the SMS as, by that time, she had decided to move to a distant suburb to live with her mother and to complete her SSC privately.

Rubina's family life was difficult, as her parents divorced when she was very young. She was living with her father Rafiq and his second wife and their children when she acted in *Slumdog Millionaire*. While she enjoyed the fame she acquired, she never completely felt a part of her father's family. After the film was made, the director Danny Boyle, and the producer Christian Colson, set up a trust called the 'Jai Ho Trust' for the two children. One of the first things they did was provide the children with more stable homes. Both had been living in a large slum community in Bandra East and moving to a nice, clean flat was a godsend to them. When Rubina was in primary school, she lived in a flat with her father and his family. After completing her primary education, she moved to her mother's home in Nallasopara, a distant suburb of Mumbai. I last met her mother Khurshid while boarding a train, and she told me sadly, *"Rubina abhi mere saath nahin reheti. Ghar chodke gai aur apni saheli ke sath reh rahi hai. College ja rahi hai aur arts pad rahi hai."* (Rubina no longer lives with me. She left home and now lives with a friend, and is studying arts in college).

Today, Rubina is very grateful to Danny Boyle, whom both she and Azhar fondly refer to as "Danny Uncle". What is heartening is that she completed her college education. She also has a great desire to do a course in acting so that she can take it up as a career. In 2020, one of the trustees of the Jai Ho Trust, which has now wound up as the children are no longer minors, told me, "Rubina is now doing very well for herself as a makeup consultant to high-end customers. She has rented a flat where she lives with her brother. She still aspires to enter the film industry at some stage, but it's not easy." She added, "Unfortunately, her father passed away about six months ago."

Azhar lost his father soon after *Slumdog Millionaire* won the Oscars and his mother became his anchor and guide. They moved into a flat at Santacruz, but the doting mother did not encourage Azhar to complete his schooling, leading him to ultimately drop out of school. Efforts by us and also the trustees of the Jai Ho Trust to get Azhar to take up a vocational course, or any course that interested him, led nowhere.

Soon after *Slumdog Millionaire* won the Oscars, Danny Boyle and Christian Colson visited our school to ensure both children received a good education. They continued to meet Rubina and Azhar and their parents almost every year when they were in school, together with the trustees of Jai Ho Trust, and were genuinely interested in the welfare of these two youngsters.

The *New York Daily News* reported Danny Boyle saying, "It's becoming a full-time job dealing with the daily hassle. I'm glad we did it, even with all the headaches." He hoped to give the children an education rather than a jackpot, what he calls, "a slow maturing" instead of a "sudden dash for glory". "Moviemaking is distorting. The last thing you want to do is turn them into a star."

At Aseema, we had done everything possible to give these two lovely youngsters as balanced and happy an upbringing as possible. Ultimately, it is in each child's hands to decide his or her own future and destiny, and it is our sincere hope that both find their own way to a meaningful and fulfilling life.

I vividly remember what little Azhar had once told me when I met him in the school corridor soon after the summer vacation. "Hello, Azhar. I do hope you had a nice vacation," I greeted him. "Yes teacher," he happily replied. "I was in London acting in a movie with Sir Anthony Hopkins." It is not every day that one hears this from our children. As he playfully joined his friends, all I could think of was, "God bless him!"

09

Another Municipal School and the Umeed Project

"Teacher, why is the sky blue?"

The director and producer of *Slumdog Millionaire*, Danny Boyle, and Christian Colson respectively, wanted to do something more than just set up the Jai Ho Trust for Rubina and Azhar. They wanted to help the children who lived in the Bandra East areas of Kherwadi, Khernagar, and Behrampada. So, they approached the NGO Plan International with a mandate to focus on four areas of the children's lives—health, education, livelihood, and advocacy. Four NGOs were selected to work on the different areas, with Aseema being asked to work on education. The project was called the 'Umeed Project', a project of hope.

We were happy and excited to be part of this initiative. Danny Boyle and Christian Colson had visited our school a couple of times and we found them to be caring, encouraging, and down to earth. Plan International launched its Indian chapter, Plan India, soon thereafter. We believed that by being part of this project, we would learn a lot about setting up systems and processes from a well-established organisation like them.

We decided to follow the same model as previously and identified an MCGM School in Bandra East, the Kherwadi Municipal School (KMS). This was a Mumbai Public School (MPS) which, in 2010, went up to Grade 4. The condition of the building was deplorable and the quality of education was poor. It didn't yet need "a miracle to hold the structure together," but if not looked after, it soon would!

At the time, I was a member of the MCGM's School Infrastructure Committee that had been appointed by the High Court, so I brought the building to the notice of the MCGM authorities. After all the legal formalities required for repairs were completed, a contractor was appointed and repairs started. The work went on for several years and almost three crores (USD 400,000) were spent on the project by the MCGM. While the repair work was not of the best quality, the school looked much more cheerful and welcoming than it had previously.

We also required trained teachers, and hiring Montessori teachers was difficult. There is only one Montessori training institute in Mumbai—the Ratan Tata Institute (RTI), which is affiliated with the Association Montessori International (AMI) in Amsterdam. The number of students that successfully complete the course each year is about 30 to 40. Not all of them take up teaching and those who do, prefer to join elite Montessori schools for well-to-do students. That puts an organisation like Aseema at a great disadvantage as we have complete Montessori environments and it is critical that we get trained teachers. This is very important as every Montessori apparatus is designed for a specific purpose and a Montessori directress (teacher) is specially trained to use the apparatus.

So, the next challenge was getting trained teachers. At the Kherwadi school, we had to find Montessori teachers for three classes: What were we going to do? It is said that God answers every earnest and sincere request of a true seeker, so in addition to making the effort to find teachers, we decided to make such a request.

We invited applications from those who would like to be trained as Montessori teachers. At exactly this time, Shalini Modi moved with her family to Mumbai. She had been trained at the Indian Montessori Centre in Chennai and also at the Kent and Sussex Montessori Centre, U.K. While she was not officially a trainer, we believed she had both the experience and the maturity to undertake the training of the group of 20 women who had applied. We then started a six-month training programme at Aseema. It was very well conducted by Shalini and her assistant Jaya Glory and, after six months of intensive training, we absorbed some of these trainees into our school. Together with the trained AMI teachers that we had, we were now all set to start three Montessori classes. Later, many of the teachers we had trained went on and completed the AMI Course with financial assistance from Aseema.

We asked Geeta Subhedar, one of our best Montessori teachers at the Santacruz school, to head KMS, and today, the school runs from kindergarten to Grade 10 under her able leadership. It is located in the middle of a huge slum and has developed the reputation of being one of the best schools in the area. Hence, the number of students seeking admission each year is more than we can accommodate. Every June (which is the start of the academic year in state board schools in Maharashtra) there is a long line of parents outside the school. Local politicians also make frequent visits and at times put tremendous pressure on us for admissions. Every year, we have to get help from the police to manage the large crowds during the admission process. Our criteria for admission remain clear and transparent—the family must be economically disadvantaged, stay within a kilometre of the school, and preference is given to those who already have one sibling in the school.

The 'Plan Project' as we call it, went on for five years. We learned to work collaboratively with the other three partners, but, of course, our focus remained on quality and value-based education. We also learned about setting up systems and processes from Plan and benefited from that learning. After five years, the project came to an end, and we had to look for other donors. When we first entered the school, the number of children was about 250, and today it is more than 1,600, with four divisions in many classes.

The challenges at this school are many. Several new teachers who have just finished their Bachelors in Education (B.Ed.) are not happy with the location of the school being so close to a slum and hence choose not to work here. The access to the school is messy and chaotic and while we have succeeded in removing the public toilet, which was just outside, the environment is not the most pleasant. During the monsoon, the entire area floods and the water sometimes enters the ground-floor classrooms. There continues to be a serious problem with the drainage of the area, and, despite many complaints, the problem has not been permanently solved. Despite major infrastructure repair work carried out some years ago, there is serious water seepage in the building, leading to the plaster falling and the paint peeling.

Student reading

And yet, despite these difficulties, this school has the maximum number of children, teachers and other staff. It is vibrant with the Aseema education approach being followed to its fullest. Geeta and her committed team do their best to see that the children learn creatively and participate in all co-curricular activities. The school has won many medals in sports, judo and art, and above all, the fact that the children love their school can be seen by its high attendance rates—90% and above. We are thrilled to bits when children ask, "Teacher, why is the sky blue?" or conduct surveys in the community on child rights or hold seminars in school on the Universal Declaration of Human Rights and the Indian Constitution.

The Pyramid – a sports class in progress

For us, what is important is that the children we educate grow up to be truly good people who stand for the truth, unafraid to stand by their conscience and principles, even if that means making nonconformist decisions. Most importantly, people who find kindness in their hearts and give selflessly.

10

The Harmony Years

Our day with Mrs Tina Ambani in Ahmedabad.

Mrs Tina Ambani's visit to Aseema and PCMS was a godsend! In early 2002, Mrs Ambani, together with the curator of her Harmony Show, Vikram Sethi from the Art Trust, visited Aseema. She had been organising the 'Harmony Show' for many years. It gave young aspiring artists from all over India a chance to display their art, together with masters like S.H. Raza and M.F. Hussain. In 2002, for the seventh Harmony Show, Tina Ambani wanted to do something different—she wanted her show to have a new social dimension. In her own words, "... I have been wondering for some time now how the Harmony Show can be made more meaningful. There has always been one thing that has been very close to my heart, which is the support of causes dedicated to easing or bettering the circumstances of those who are less privileged than some of us."

Mrs Ambani and Vikram Sethi visited our office one morning in January 2002. We were very excited—she was the wife of one of the wealthiest men in India and also equally well known for being one of the prettiest and finest actresses of her time. With Varsha Trivedi, our art teacher, Nicola Dadyburjor, our pre-primary head, and Millie Mitra, a dedicated volunteer, I met them in our office in Bandra. Varsha showed Mrs Ambani the children's art and explained how we worked. Mrs Ambani seemed at ease in our little office and liked what she saw. We told her about our newly "adopted" school and she immediately said, "I would like to see the school right away." We drove off in her Mercedes to PCMS, which is close to our office, and showed her around the school. I was unsure whether I should take her into one of the much-discussed toilets but took my chance and did. She quietly observed the broken pipes, the rusted shelves and the overall shabby environment and left the school, saying, "I will be in touch."

That evening when I got home, there was a message on my answering machine asking me to call her back. I didn't waste a moment and immediately did. "I am very interested in your work and will send someone to discuss the matter with you," she said. Then added, "Besides the Harmony Show, I would like to assist in many other ways." I immediately shared the good news with my niece Armeen, who lived with me at the time and we danced a little jig, such was our joy! The next few calls were to Varsha, Nicola, Millie, and, of course, Snehal and Neela.

A few days later, we had Mr Arun Bhende, the CEO of the Dhirubhai Ambani Foundation, visit us to learn more about our work. He and his colleagues from the foundation went through our records and documents and were satisfied.

Soon thereafter Mrs Ambani called, "I am going to my office in Ahmedabad tomorrow and am also visiting the National Institute of Design (NID) there," she said and added, "and I want you to accompany me." My head reeled, and I replied, "I need to think about it," not realising that I had done the unthinkable. Mrs Ambani calmly replied, "I won't take no for an answer, and do bring along anyone you want. Also, please carry some of your children's art to show to my team in Ahmedabad." When I relayed this to a well-wisher of Aseema who moves around in such circles, she exclaimed, "No one talks like that to Mrs Ambani, you must go!" In a daze, I called Varsha. "We have to go with Mrs Ambani to Ahmedabad tomorrow. She wants us to go to her office there and also to the famous design institute, NID." Varsha's reaction was similar to mine. After it had all sunk in, we got busy; there was so much to do!

The next morning, when Varsha and I reached the airport, Mrs Ambani was already there and in a great hurry. The children's art that we were carrying and all of us were whisked aboard her beautiful private aircraft. Breakfast was served and Mrs Ambani was friendly and chatted with us throughout the short and pleasant flight. Soon, we were in Ahmedabad where her team, headed by Mr K. Narayan, President of Reliance Industries, Textile Division, was waiting for us. She greeted them all very warmly and introduced Mr Narayan as "my boss". We drove to NID and had a whirlwind tour of the lovely institute. Varsha and I quietly sat through a meeting with the director, the faculty, a few students, Mrs Ambani and Mr Narayan.

Another car ride and we were at her office where we broke up into two groups—Mrs Ambani with the NID folks and Varsha and I with Ashwini, Minnie, and some of their colleagues from Mrs Ambani's office. Things immediately slowed down; we had a lovely *thali* lunch in their cafeteria and got to know each other better. After lunch and a tour of their office, we sat down to talk about Aseema. Ashwini, we learnt, was the person who handled the Harmony Show, and he was the person we were to deal with. Minnie was the person in charge of communications and she asked a lot of questions: how and why we had started Aseema, where the children came from, what our goal for them was, and so on. They were joined by their creative team, who were amazed to see the children's art. "You mean the children have done this!" they exclaimed. Varsha would immediately reply, "Yes, they have learnt about different masks made all over the world," and then give details about the differences and similarities between the masks of Fiji, Venice, Africa, and India. Everyone listened with rapt attention as Varsha went on to explain our other projects—Australian aboriginal art, Wycinanki, the Polish art of paper cutting, and so on. Everyone was warm and friendly and very interested in Aseema's work.

Mrs Ambani and Mr Narayan joined us later and Aseema's place in the Harmony Show was firmed up. I remember being very excited and also a little intimidated, wondering what was going to happen next. It was very comforting to have Varsha by my side. Then it was action time once again, rushing to the airport, to Mumbai, and finally back home! It had been a long and tiring day, but we knew we had to share all that had happened with our families and friends. Everyone wanted to know how we had spent our day with the famous Mrs Ambani.

11

The Harmony Show and Other Art Exhibitions

"If you invest in beauty, it will remain with you all the days of your life."

– Frank Lloyd Wright

Then began the hectic preparations for the Harmony Show, 2002. Fortunately, we had collected a lot of the children's art since Varsha's classes had commenced at Aseema.

Varsha with a student in the art class

I had known Varsha since I was in school. She was a good friend of my sister, Arnavaz. Besides being a very fine artist and a gold medallist from the Sir J.J. School of Art, Mumbai, Varsha was not only a wonderful art teacher but also a wonderful human being—warm and friendly, caring and compassionate. She had been a volunteer at Aseema, teaching the children at our centre at St. Stanislaus since June 1999.

It was initially very difficult getting Varsha to teach at Aseema. "I know that you are an excellent art teacher with years of experience. Please come and teach our children," I pleaded on several occasions. Finally, she came over one morning to my home and gave me lots of beautiful cards she had made working with children at a school for the deaf. "Do sell these so that you can raise some money for Aseema," she said, but mentioned nothing about teaching our children. I was very disappointed but did not give up. After a while, things worked out by themselves with the Inner Wheel Club of Mumbai West supporting the art programme at Aseema and Varsha, as a member of the club, coming on board to conduct the art class. I was very happy, and the children were delighted! Varsha had more than 30 years of teaching experience and was wonderful with the children.

Not only did she make the art class come alive with Australian Aboriginal art, Warli art, impressionist art, mask art, and African textile art but she also took the children in their imagination to different parts of the world. Most important was the way she interacted with them. She treated them with so much respect that they not only loved her but also gave her their very best. The art that the children produced then, and continue to produce under her guidance, enthrals us to this day. What's more, the days she and Rita Shroff, another volunteer from the Inner Wheel Club came by; they would bring the children a delicious snack which made them love her even more!

In August 1999, we participated in our very first art exhibition, organised by the Concern India Foundation (CIF). The exhibition was at South Mumbai's well-known Cymroza Art Gallery. CIF was a funding agency, and they asked each of the organisations they supported to contribute ten paintings, which they would frame and hopefully sell. Varsha had started working with the children only a short time before this exhibition and neither she nor we had any idea of how the children would perform. Fortunately, all ten of the paintings we gave CIF sold instantly. More significant was the impact it had on our children. The organisers had invited a small group of them to the opening, and I will never forget the look of pure delight on their faces when they entered the gallery and saw their paintings so prominently displayed!

We participated in the Harmony Show three years later and the art improved with each passing year. We had a wonderful collection of about 200 paintings on display at the 2002 Harmony Show, and also a lovely collection of products that were made from children's art.

Ashwini from Mrs Ambani's office worked closely with our team and assisted us with organising the entire event—invaluable help as it was all very new to us and on such a large scale. The art gallery at the Nehru Centre was given to us to display our work, and it took us five days to set it up with many of our friends and family pitching in.

Mrs Tina Ambani came to the school a few days before the show to meet the children, accompanied by her photographer. "Please bring the children for lunch on the opening day," she said, "I want them to have a good time." A wonderful spread was laid out for the children and staff at the Nehru Centre Garden, not just that year, but every year that we participated in the show, seven in all.

The show opened on April 6, 2002, and was a huge success! The children's art was greatly appreciated and a lot of interest was generated in the work Aseema was doing. Seeing their work share the same space with artists from all over the country gave a boost to the children's self-esteem. The exhibition catalogue mentioned the names of the child artists, together with their work, alongside the names of all the other artists participating in the show, which really excited the children and all of us. Very thoughtfully, Mrs Ambani had a few Aseema children standing alongside her own children and

Mrs Mrinalini Sarabai, the chief guest, as she lit the inaugural lamp. "Come along," she insisted, "you all must be there too."

While only a few children came to the evening opening ceremony, which was attended by the who's who of Mumbai, all the children, together with their parents, were brought to see the exhibition on another day. This practice continued all the years that we were part of the show.

Besides the entire Ambani family, celebrities like Julio Rebeiro, a well-respected former Police Commissioner of Mumbai, Shobhaa De, the popular novelist and columnist, and Parmeshwar Godrej, philanthropist and socialite also attended the show. Among the guests every year were actor Amitabh Bachchan, his wife Jaya Bachchan, their son Abhishek Bachchan, and his wife, Aishwarya Rai Bachchan. Also present were philanthropist Rajeshwari Birla, and politician Uddhav Thackeray.

Mrs Ambani would always bring them to see our children's art, and many of them bought paintings and products. I remember Jaya Bachchan buying several paintings. These celebrities usually attended the opening night, and it was very exciting for our children to see them all. Whenever they saw a famous actor or actress, they would come running to tell us, "Teacher, teacher, Aishwarya Rai has come... she is so beautiful, looks like a mermaid!"

It was exciting for us as well. The opening night was always full of glitz and glamour—cocktails and delicious delicacies and we would be exhausted by the end of it. Most important for us was that sales should be good and on the opening night, they always were.

I often wondered what impact this had on our children and considered it our duty to keep them as grounded as possible. They were still very young, and for them, it was all about enjoying themselves and having a good time. For us adults, it was a little more complicated. The full-page advertisements in the leading newspapers would announce

'Harmony Supports Aseema'. Many people, including some of the regular Aseema donors, took it to mean that all of Aseema's financial troubles were over. Here was Mrs Ambani who would take care of all of Aseema's finances. To be fair to Mrs Ambani, she had never promised us anything of the sort. Yes, she had promised us a platform at the Harmony Show, which gave us tremendous visibility, but that was it. She also helped in repairing and renovating the Pali Chimbai Municipal School and sent her team to work on the washrooms, toilets, drainage system, and playground. This enabled us to create an environment at the school that was pleasant and conducive to learning.

I remember my surprise and disappointment, when one donor who had been supporting Aseema said, "Please can I have my cheque back? You will not need my help any longer." No amount of explanation or persuasion could make them understand that financially Aseema was still in the same situation that it had been before the Harmony Show. At the beginning of every academic year, we are still unsure of whether we will be able to meet our budgets and expenses for the year.

When asked why she had chosen Aseema over other organisations that were doing similar work and had been around much longer, Mrs Ambani replied, "I was amazed at the wonderful work that they have been doing. Also, they are barely four years old and, in a way, we are trying to help an upcoming NGO establish itself. It is in sync with Harmony's ideology."

The 2002 show lasted eight days, and it became an event that all the children and the entire Aseema team looked forward to with great enthusiasm. Though the show was always held in early April, by January itself the children would ask, "When is the Harmony Show, teacher? When will we be going to the Nehru Centre?" In the subsequent years, our paintings and products were displayed in the gallery just outside the main halls where the artists' works were exhibited.

There was much disappointment when seven years later we were no longer part of the show. This eventually led to Aseema organising its exhibition at the Cymroza Art Gallery in September 2011.

At the Cymroza exhibition of 2011, almost all the art was put together by nine of the Aseema alumni. These were children who had worked with Varsha for more than 10 years and many were now in college and even working part time. The exhibition was beautiful and all the visitors were amazed at what the children were capable of doing. Sales were very good as well, and it generated more revenue than all our other exhibitions held so far. It was also the first exhibition where a part of the sale proceeds were given to the alumni. After giving them their share, we asked them what the surplus amount should be used for, and they unanimously declared that it should go towards Aseema's Art Programme. "We would like all the children of the school to learn art the way we have," they said. This goes to show the impact the art classes and the product division have had on these young minds. It also showed that each one of us, no matter how young, is capable of giving to others. It spoke volumes about their generosity, of wanting to give back what was so precious to them.

Another exhibition worth mentioning took place in 2005 at the JW Marriott Hotel at Juhu in Mumbai. To support Aseema, the hotel provided us with a wonderful display area in their shopping zone. When we first saw the display window, we were completely bowled over! I immediately called both Varsha and Nicola, "Hello! This is amazing, but I don't know where to begin, and how to get it all organised. Can you please help?" It was huge, in a prominent location, and one of the most beautiful hotels in Mumbai. With Varsha and Nicola's help, we set up an artistic display of all our products, which were to be sold from their popular coffee shop, the Bombay Baking Company (BBC).

The general manager at the time, John Webb, was very supportive and suggested we have a five-day exhibition in the hotel. Delighted, we immediately agreed! The staff of the hotel was extremely cooperative and the best of props and lights were provided. Varsha and Armeen, my niece (who was Aseema's product manager at the time), worked hard with our support staff, Munni and Vinayak, and some of our older students to put up what was perhaps our most beautiful exhibition ever. John wanted the show to be attended by many of his guests, so Aseema was given only 50 invitations to the opening. We were in a dilemma as to who to invite. We finally drew up a list of 50, and the rest were invited for the remaining four days of the show.

On the morning of the opening, some of us went to the hotel and were stunned by the display, it was spectacular! The huge collages of the elements of nature—earth, water, fire, air, and space stole the show. Even those of us who had seen the work in progress in the art class found it hard to believe that the children had created these spectacular works. A new addition to the show was two papier mâché goats made by Bhagvan Kaddu, a tribal artist from Jawhar, (a village in Maharashtra), on which our children had painted works inspired by Miro, Matisse, and Paul Klee. Also new were a series of bowls and plates made and painted by the children. Ramesh Ghayal, one of our older and most talented boys, had been sent by Varsha to learn papier mâché and had made lovely bowls that the younger children had painted. We left the hotel, confident that the show would be a resounding success.

The opening was at 7:00 p.m. and John had done everything in style. Care had been taken to organise the best cocktails, drinks, and aperitives for the guests. But the only guests who came that day were the 50 that Aseema had invited. There were no other guests, not a single other person. John, of course, was there and was very gracious. All those at Aseema who had taken great pains to put up this beautiful exhibition enjoyed the hospitality of JW Marriott, and each other's company, but were sorely disappointed that, apart from our friends and guests, no one saw the show that night.

To this day, we wonder what happened to the 200 beautifully designed invitations John sent his esteemed guests. For the remaining four days of the show, we invited everyone we knew to come and see the children's work and, of course, as with every other exhibition, all the children and their parents also came to the show. Over the next four days, JW Marriott continued to be generous and hospitable, for which we will always be grateful.

A year later, we discovered to our great dismay that our lovely products had been removed from the big display window outside the BBC to make way for a leading "designer". We realised it was time for us to move on, but we look back on the years we took our friends to see that beautiful display window, with great pride and happiness.

12

More Exhibitions

NGO Mela of the Concern India Foundation;
Ladies Wing, Indian Merchants Chamber;
American Tourister—Dream Destinations,
and Global Desi.

Aseema had been taking part in the NGO mela (fair) organised by the Concern India Foundation for many years. The mela was initially held on the Cricket Club of India (CCI) grounds at Churchgate in South Mumbai. Organisations and craftsmen came from all parts of India and it was an interesting and fun place. We usually sold all the items we had on display, which at the time were few and basic—handmade greeting cards, wrapping paper, and painted lanterns. The volunteers who helped always had a lot of fun. Our children would put up a judo display on one of the evenings and eagerly looked forward to the event.

The first time Cavas Billimoria, the judo Arjuna Award winner, saw our children perform at the event, he said, "Your children have no fear. See how they fly... they will go far." Cavas had one of his judo instructors come to Aseema to train our children. They have been learning judo in school for many years now, and have won numerous awards and medals.

It was Arti Vakil, an Aseema well-wisher, who introduced us to Cavas. Arti also put us in touch with the ladies wing of the Indian Merchants Chamber (IMC). They organised a big exhibition every year to which they invited women entrepreneurs. Many well-to-do women came to the exhibition and shopped till they dropped. It was a perfect place for Aseema to have a stall. In 2000, SoulKurry.com, a start-up, wanted to sponsor four NGOs to this event in the hope that it would create awareness about their work and also help generate revenue. Since Aseema's product range was very limited at the time, with only cards and a few craft items, we quickly got ready for what promised to be quite a grand affair.

We decided to meet at the home of another Aseema well-wisher, Shital Mehta. "Let's have a brainstorming session to discuss how we could add to the Aseema product range," suggested Shital. Besides being a graphic artist and a superb art teacher, Shital made the most excellent pani puri and bhel puri (popular street food in Mumbai). So over platefuls of bhel and pani puri, Varsha, Arti, Shital's daughter Laher, her niece Urmee, and a group of us from Aseema, discussed what we should do in the short time available. We then dived into all that the children had done in their art class in the past few years. "Take a look at these paintings. I can't wait to show you everything!" Varsha said excitedly, displaying the art done by the children all over the floor in Shital's huge living room. "They are marvellous! I can confidently say we must make art books, gift envelopes, and lamps," declared Shital. Together with her talented niece and daughter, she came up with some very creative ideas, and the next few weeks were spent looking for the right vendors. Samples were made and approved, and final orders were placed.

The IMC Ladies Wing exhibition was at Bajaj Bhavan at Nariman Point, Mumbai, for two days. Since we shared a stall with three other NGOs, space was limited. It is expected that NGOs will cooperate and help one another, but, as experience has shown, they can also be very competitive! So, there was a little bit of pushing and pulling and squabbling about space and we decided to keep only a limited amount of stock under the table we were sharing with the others. Soon, the women descended on us and we were only able to cope as we had two very efficient volunteers manning our stall—Monika Koller, a young

Swiss lady who was stationed in Mumbai for six months, and my sister-in-law Tannaz.

Our products were hugely popular, and we were soon running out of stock. Our art books and gift envelopes were a big hit. We called for more from the vendor but had no place to make sets of envelopes. "Let's just sit on the steps at the entrance to the hall," declared Monika enthusiastically, "And make hay while the sun shines!" As soon as the stocks arrived, the two of us sat on the steps of Bajaj Bhavan packing the gift envelopes, which were selling like hotcakes, even as beautiful ladies in their marvellous attire and exquisite jewellery looked on curiously.

The next day, the organisation we were sharing the table with decided to give the exhibition a miss, so we were able to display our products more comfortably. This exhibition gave us the idea and the confidence to do something more with the beautiful art of our children. It was the starting point of what would finally lead to the creation of our product division.

Over the next few years, we participated in several exhibitions, including one at the popular Zenzi Restaurant in Bandra, in 2007. The international advertising agency, TBWA, had commissioned art for the American Tourister luggage brand. The children were asked to create their "dream destinations". A difficult task, given that almost none of them had travelled out of their communities, let alone Bandra and Mumbai! The art teacher who worked with them at the time was Amit Romani, a young artist, very talented and sure of himself. He showed the children pictures of tourist landmarks and their creativity flowed. Two artworks were finally selected—a painting of the Statue of Liberty in the US and the Burj Al Arab Hotel in Dubai. These were used in the company's limited edition luggage collection and were part of its marketing campaign.

Art commissioned for the American Tourister Luggage brand –
The Statue of Liberty in USA

Art commissioned for the American Tourister Luggage brand –
Burj Al Arab Hotel in Dubai

At the launch of the collection, well-known fashion designers like Anita Dongre also put the children's art on scarves, which together with the Aseema products and paintings, were sold at the Zenzi exhibition. The exhibition was a huge success with almost all the paintings being sold along with many products.

But the biggest excitement of all was having the most popular actor in India, Salman Khan, and his sister Alvira Agnihotri attend the exhibition! He went on to buy many of the paintings and products and spoke to the children at length. Despite running a fever and being under the weather that evening, he put in an appearance wearing a blue bandanna and casual t-shirt and stole the show.

"Do tell me how you have done all these paintings," he asked the two boys whose paintings had been selected, putting his arm around them. It no longer mattered to the children whether their paintings sold or not—that their hero had come and interacted with them meant the world to them.

Anita Dongre, who had designed some of the scarves and stoles for the Zenzi exhibition, later approached us for other art done by our students. In 2010, she introduced a special line for her brand Global Desi with 15 designs created out of a colourful series of paintings on elephants done by the children. In 2012, she selected another set of art—Australian Aboriginal designs and launched the 'Global Desi in Support of Aseema' collection where the paintings were put on tops and kurtis. The Aseema children were invited to the launch of the collection at the Palladium, Phoenix Mills at Lower Parel in Mumbai, and were delighted to see their art on the stylish tunics.

Apart from the above exhibitions, many corporates, schools, and a few hotels and restaurants invite us each year, particularly around festivals, to display and sell our products and we invariably have good sales.

While the amount generated from the sale of products is still minimal, the interest it generates in our core work—education—makes the entire exercise of running a product division worthwhile. Also, the sense of fulfilment and happiness that the Aseema children experience every time they see their art displayed and sold does wonders for their self-esteem.

Salman Khan with two budding child artists

13

The Establishment of the Product Division

We do not want people to buy the Aseema products out of sympathy or simply for charity. We would like them to be bought because they are works of art by some remarkable children.

It was August 2002, and I was at home one morning when the phone rang. It was the time when landlines were still in use. The person at the other end said, "Hi! Is this Dilbur Parakh?" "Yes, it is," I replied. "Are you the Dilbur Parakh who studied at St. Xavier's College years ago?" It was Mukul Pandya, a college friend who had gone on to become a journalist at *The Times of India*, Mumbai, and then moved to the United States of America, after which I lost touch with him.

Mukul had been one of the cleverest students of our college, the prestigious St. Xavier's in South Mumbai, run by the Jesuits. After the initial excitement of catching up after almost 20 years, he mentioned that he was now the editor and director of *Knowledge@Wharton*, the online journal of the Wharton School of the University of Pennsylvania. "I have seen the Aseema website and would really like to know more about the art done by your students and the products that you make from their art," he said and went on, "I recognise the potential of your students and think your product division will benefit from a business input." It was wonderful to hear this from him, as I had long felt that we had not been able to do justice to our children's art. "I would like to explore the possibility of the students of the Wharton Business School studying your initiative and putting together a business plan for you." It sounded too good to be true, and we exchanged information and notes to take the matter forward.

After detailed discussions, the Aseema-Knowledge@Wharton initiative was started with another well-known management college in Mumbai—the S.P. Jain Institute of Management and Research, joining in as well.

For three years, from 2003 to 2005, the students of the Wharton Business School worked together with the students of the S.P. Jain Institute. The Wharton teams had interesting names: Team Magnum, Team SKID, and The Bombay Squad. At the end of every year, their reports were discussed at a video conference held at the S.P. Jain Institute, which was attended by both teams, the Aseema students and those of us involved in developing the art and products, as well as by the students and faculty from both the business schools.

The reports were detailed and discussed steps towards Aseema becoming a self-sustaining entity. The division of labour was like this: While the Wharton students explored the demand side and potential marketing channels for Aseema products, the students from S.P Jain focused on the supply side and potential challenges. How Aseema could use the e-commerce market through their new website was also studied. Based in Mumbai, the students from the S.P. Jain Institute—Raj Roy, Umesh Nayak, Shweta Singh, Mrinal Singh, Ankur Garg, and Amita Khattri—interacted regularly with Aseema team members and made many useful suggestions.

It was a great learning opportunity for all of us at Aseema, and I am sure for the students of both the business schools as well. This, together with the exhibitions we had taken part in over the years, made us realise that it was time for us now to professionalise our products. It could and should no longer be handled by only the teachers, volunteers, and office staff. We looked for a product manager and finally, the product division at Aseema was born.

Mr. Behram Sabawala, CFO of Tata International, and his young enthusiastic team provided invaluable support and guidance to us at this critical time as we worked on strengthening the Product Division.

What is important to note is that it was possible to set up the product division because the art being done in the schools was of a very high quality. As in all other schools, there was an art period for every class and all the children took part in this. Then there were children who were naturally gifted and very interested in art; it was for them that the Room 13 Art Studio was set up.

The Room 13 movement, initiated by Rob Wright and Claire, started in 1994 in a primary school in the West Highlands of Scotland. The students of the school had an art studio where they would paint, undertake research, read, and discuss things with the artist-in-residence. It was their room, managed entirely by them. In a short span of time, Room 13 became a network of such studios worldwide, host to a growing international movement of young artists.

When Aseema's well-wishers, Mary and Peter Ashton, watched a documentary in London on Room 13 broadcast on the BBC, *What Age Can You Start Being an Artist?*, they immediately thought of Aseema. The Ashtons had supported Aseema's work over the years and put us in touch with Claire. Mary wrote to say, "We saw this wonderful programme on the BBC about a school in Scotland and their art programme, and immediately thought of Aseema. I am going to put you in touch with them right away."

She did, and we took it further. We got in touch with Claire, who referred us to the advertising agency TBWA, Mumbai, and with their assistance, we were able to start a Room 13 studio at our Pali Chimbai Municipal School in August 2006. The studio was inaugurated by Mr Bazlur Rehman, education officer of the MCGM, who was particularly happy that such an initiative was being undertaken in an MCGM school. Kurien Matthews, the then CEO of TBWA, and his colleagues were a great support in setting up the studio.

Before the formal inauguration, a group of students from Room 13 in Scotland and England together with Claire visited our art studio, and this is what Kerrie Grant, one of the students, wrote in a 2005 Room 13 Annual Report, "We were met by two women and after chatting about Room 13, we discovered Mrs Ashton was dead right! We all found the atmosphere at Aseema wonderfully similar to Room 13 and felt completely at home there." She went on to add, "I got a lot from my experience in India, especially when we were at the school. I found out how different my culture is from theirs and that many people live in poverty. Overall, my experience was worthwhile, and I got a lot from it. That's the good thing about Room 13—you get so many opportunities and chances to see new things and freedom to express yourself."

The basic philosophy of Room 13 is that art is not 'taught', but is a unique expression of an individual child artist. Children work as co-artists with the artist-in-residence. While Aseema does not have 'artists-in-residence', we do have some very fine art teachers and artists who work with the children and introduce them to the work of different artists and techniques. The wonderful art library, built up over the years, encourages the children to explore and expand their horizons. And then, of course, there is the internet, which brings art from all over the world into the art studio and classrooms! The children are also taken to art exhibitions held at leading art galleries, and from time to time, visiting artists are invited to work with them. In recent years, some children have attended long-term art courses where they have worked side by side with established artists.

Over the years, our Room 13 Art Studio students have become acquainted with Warli and Gond Art, Kalighat painting, Madhubani, and works by Indian masters like Raza, M.F. Husain, Sakti Burman, and Jamini Roy. They have also studied Australian Aboriginal art, and the work of European artists like Van Gogh, Henri Rousseau, Claude Monet, and Henri Matisse. They particularly enjoyed studying the Sri Lankan artist Senaka Senanayake's forest and flower forms and have also learnt scratch art, the marbling technique, and the Polish art of intricate paper cutting, Wycinanki. A great favourite with them was also Tinga-Tinga, a style of art that emerged in the twentieth century in Dar-es-Salaam, Tanzania. Besides the technique used by the artist, the children also learn about the artists, their lives, and the countries they come from.

In 2013, our students worked on the illustrations for a children's book on human rights entitled, *The Right to Be* written by Ms. Zina Sorabjee. A young graphic art designer, Sabina, guided our children over the summer vacation. Once the illustrations were done, our art teachers and all of us were amazed to see the work the children produced. It was not an easy task, but they persevered, and as the author herself acknowledged in the book, "Without their paintings, the book would have lost much of its attraction."

Some years later, our students were asked once again to illustrate a children's storybook by Tulika Maheshwari titled *Sashu Padhi Kashu*, once again with stunning results.

Product Division

Today, our art team has grown, and besides Varsha, we have art teachers in all our schools. Farida Ahmad, who heads the Room 13 Art Studio at the Pali Chimbai Municipal School, has been teaching art to children for many years. Her detailed and meticulous preparation for an art class is really very special. She researches every topic so thoroughly that the children actually feel and experience it.

Varsha and Farida select the best art done by the students every quarter and send these paintings to Aseema's product division.

A design team meeting is held every year and is eagerly looked forward to. As we review one sample after another, there is much excitement all around! "Oh, this is beautiful! The art is stunning, but I don't think it lends itself to this tray." Or, "This is the best product we ever had!" Sometimes we find the price too low and sometimes too high. We don't always agree on the product or the design, and then there is a lot of discussion and finally, a solution is found.

The Aseema products include:

- Stationery like greeting cards, gift tags, gift envelopes, and calendars.
- Cloth bags and other kinds of handbags, purses, wallets, and toilet pouches.
- Wooden items like pencil boxes, boxes in different shapes and sizes, trays of all sizes and office stationery sets.
- Glasses, mugs of all shapes and sizes, and candle holders.
- Coasters, trivets, laptop bags, and suitcase tags.
- Three-dimensional objects made or painted by the older children like jars (*bharnis*), goats, turtles, owls, elephants, and masks made with papier mâché or other material, all exquisitely painted or with decoupage.

Aseema is supported primarily through private philanthropy, and more recently, through corporate social responsibility (CSR). We have been trying to supplement our resources with the revenue generated through the sale of our products. It has always been our hope to generate sufficient income from the sale of our children's art and products to enable us to run our schools and continue our work. Today, most of our funding comes from corporates, other trusts and foundations, and individual donors. As the number of students and staff at Aseema increases, it is crucial that we consider other avenues for generating income, which will make us more self-sufficient.

It has not been easy running the product division. A huge amount of time and effort goes into sourcing suitable vendors, ensuring quality control, keeping a proper inventory, and storing the products safely. We do not have an astute business sense and attracting young people who have studied management, marketing, and sales to work at Aseema has not been possible because we cannot pay the high salaries that most of them demand. In order to bring down costs, it is important to order in bulk, which is not possible for us as we can neither block our capital to place bulk orders nor do we have enough storage space to accommodate products ordered in large quantities.

However, seeing the beautiful art that comes out of the schools and seeing the high-quality products that feature the children's art—we feel this is a most worthwhile venture and are making all efforts to strengthen our product division. We do not want people to buy Aseema products out of sympathy or simply for charity. We would like them to be bought because they are works of art by some remarkable children. We are hopeful that corporates will continue to call us to their offices for exhibitions and will continue to buy Aseema products for corporate gifting. We also call upon individuals to spread the word about Aseema products, which make wonderful gifts.

When we undertook the project with *Knowledge@Wharton* and the S.P. Jain Institute of Management, we hoped to nurture marketing and commercial skills in our students—skills that would complement the education they receive in the Aseema schools.

Another wonderful aspect of the art studio and product division is the opportunity it gives the children to see their beautiful work displayed and featured on various products. It is tremendously empowering for them to see their art being appreciated and bought. It also educates them and brings them tremendous joy to see the magnificent creations of the masters; to study their lives and techniques, and, like them, create objects of beauty and interest.

Art also has a tremendously calming influence on the children, enabling them to concentrate better. In the Room 13 studio, the child is free to discover, explore, question, and create. This is encouraged and leads to the children knowing that their thoughts and feelings matter. Most importantly, it is in keeping with Aseema's education approach—letting them know they are valued is the most empowering gift you can give a child.

14

Raju & I

"God dwells in the details."

– Mies van der Rohe

One of the first grants we received was to make a film on child rights and education. As mentioned earlier, we had appointed two researchers to study this issue: Asha Bajpai, a professor at the Tata Institute of Social Sciences (TISS), and Sangita Kamdar, an economics professor at Sophia College in Mumbai. Their report provided more data for the film and Neela started looking for a good team who could work on it.

She selected a company called Animagic run by three creative and very enthusiastic youngsters —Gayatri Rao, Sumant Rao, and Chetan Sharma. Their office at that time was on the first floor of a dilapidated building on Charni Road. When Neela took me to meet them, I noticed that the office doubled as a residence. They were so involved and passionate about their work that they spent almost all their time at the office. Their creativity seemed to flower at night, which is why it often seemed that they were up all night working on various assignments. Sometimes when we visited their office during the day and inquired after one of them who was not present, they would say he or she was asleep in the adjoining room!

Initially, it was decided that the film would take six months to complete. But they enjoyed working on our film so much that the time stretched to more than two years! It was to be an animation film and illustrations were done with pastels, frame by frame, and then loaded on the computer. The characters in the film slowly emerged—first Atul, then Raju, the *chaiwala*, the *polishwala*, the construction worker, and so on. And finally, the unfolding of the main plot. Numerous meetings were held in their office and on each visit, we were given a glimpse of each new character and scene. After about a year, we were very anxious: Was the film ever going to be completed? Every time we visited, we saw a little bit more of the work in progress... but eventually we got used to the fact that they could only work at their own highly chaotic pace!

All three were intelligent and creative, and though they gave us many sleepless nights over whether the project would be complete, I eventually grew very fond of them. Part of my admiration had to do with the passion they put into the project. Every detail was taken care of and the film was incredibly sensitively made.

It was a difficult subject, and, to be effective, ought not to be preachy. It had to be informative and interesting and also inspire and motivate the viewer. The audience was meant to be school children; the purpose was to make them aware of the reality many children in India face—poverty, the exploitation of children working in different industries, child-bonded labour, and so on. The message was meant to be one of hope and optimism; that one did not have to be a person of importance to make a difference. Everyone could do it in their own way, even a school child. The film went on to talk about the United Nations Convention on the rights of the child and the cycle of poverty that could be broken with education. Education is a force to reckon with and take seriously, was the main message.

Once completed, *Raju & I* went on to win many national and international awards, including the very prestigious National Film Award for the best animation film of 2004. I remember going to New Delhi in October 2005 to receive the award on behalf of Aseema. All three—Gayatri, Sumant, and Chetan were also there, and Gayatri received the award for directing the film. The award ceremony was at the beautiful Vigyan Bhavan and there was a full rehearsal the morning of the awards where we were all told what to do and how to go on stage to receive the award from the then President of India, Dr A.P.J. Abdul Kalam.

Receiving the National Film Award from President Abdul Kalam for 'Raju and I'

The award ceremony took place that evening and the hall was packed with many famous film personalities like Yash Chopra, the iconic Bollywood movie director and producer; Saif Ali Khan, Bollywood actor and the heir to the last Nawab of Pataudi; Madhur Bhandarkar, director and producer; and Rituparno Ghosh, a pioneering director among others. I must confess that for a while I wondered what I was doing in the midst of this gathering and wished Neela, with her film background, had been in my place instead. But when I later heard from Shobha how the little Aseema children had waited patiently in Mumbai to watch me go up on stage to receive the prestigious award from none other than one of India's most respected and popular presidents, it all seemed worthwhile. Later Shobha told me, "Teacher, we all came together to see you on TV and when you went on stage, we cheered and clapped a lot!"

We also made a calendar from stills from the film, which was hugely popular. It was commissioned by SKF, the Swedish Ball Bearing Company, which bought 35,000 calendars from Aseema. The beautiful images done by Animagic were used on the 12-page wall calendar, which was printed at Silverpoint Press, one of the best printing presses in India.

SKF confirmed the order for the calendar in late November and wanted all 35,000 copies dispatched by mid-December. Time was short, but we pleaded with Mr Saifee of Silverpoint to meet the deadline. All the Aseema calendars over the years have been printed at Silverpoint Press and he knew us well and graciously accommodated our request. It was a big order for us and it meant reaching out to 35,000 more people and also additional funding. Both were much needed.

Mr Saifee also knew that we were very particular about the colour being just right and other details, which is why we always remained present at the press when printing started. He warned us, "Since this is very urgent, we will have to fit it into our schedule somehow. So, you may have to come to the press any time we start printing; it may be in the middle of the night as well." So anxious were we to get the order that we readily agreed. Sure enough, a call would come at 1:00 or 2:00 a.m. that certain pages were being taken up for printing. I would hurriedly get ready, call the Animagic folks and all of us would trudge to Silverpoint Press. Fortunately, my sister Arnavaz was with me at the time; so she would accompany me to Lower Parel, where the press was located. This happened on at least three or four occasions while the calendar was being printed. I vividly remember how minutely Gayatri and Chetan would examine the first lot of pages when printing started under a magnifying glass to make sure that every detail and every colour came out exactly the way it should.

The calendar was one of the very best we have ever had. Working with the Animagic team and the two experiences I had, both with the film and calendar, reinforced my belief in the power of passion and the importance of focusing on the details. As they say, "God dwells in the details."

(https://www.youtube.com/watch?v=CPgMDt-soWw)

2005 National Award winner for Best Animation film and winner of 14 National and International Awards

SECTION IV

IGATPURI

15

First Visit to Igatpuri

The wishing well at the YSS Sadhnalaya takes me to Awalkhed.

The first time I went to Igatpuri was to attend a yoga retreat at the beautiful Paramahansa Yogananda Sadhnalaya (PYS) in 2003. It was with my very dear friend and former boss, Bindu Kumana, and as we drove there, Binduben chatted the entire way, telling me all about her childhood and growing up. I fell in love with the PYS as soon as I stepped onto the ground. If there was a heaven on earth, for me this was it. The feeling was inexplicable. It was very quiet and peaceful and the retreat was conducted with exceptional sensitivity. The experience made me forget all my problems and day-to-day worries, at least for the moment, and brought about a feeling of great contentment.

The Sadhnalaya had terracotta Mangalore tiled roofs and open-concept hallways. The landscaping was beautifully done and the impressive mountains in the distance were breathtaking. There was a sense of possibility in the air—of hope, freedom, and the belief that anything can be done if you want it enough. Perhaps it was the state of calm my mind was in after the retreat, but that visit seemed to open a door to ideas I dismissed a long time ago, ideas that seemed too far-fetched.

Once the retreat was over, I returned to Mumbai. But I longed to go back and very soon I returned to Igatpuri for another retreat. One morning as I was sitting near the wishing well on the hill in the Sadhnalaya garden, the thought of setting up a residential school for some of our students arose.

A couple of years before this visit, a group of teachers at Aseema had come to me with a problem. "We are doing everything possible to give our children a good education. But there are a few children who come from families that are very, very dysfunctional. There is so much abuse at home that it negates all that we do at school," they said. "We take one step forward with them in school and when they go home, they have moved two steps back. Can we not have a small residential facility for such children?" they pleaded.

I tried hard to get a small plot in Mumbai to set up a residential facility for some of the children who needed to be moved from their home environment, but the plan did not materialise. The place we were looking for had to be conducive to a child's growth and development, and there seemed to be no such place in Mumbai anymore. The city was bursting at the seams and land prices were unaffordable. For us, it was important to have a suitable building set in beautiful, inspiring, and peaceful surroundings. After a two-year search, we realised that it would be impossible to afford such a place in Mumbai.

The wishing well at the Paramahansa Yogananda Sadhnalaya

Sitting by the wishing well at the Sadhnalaya, it dawned on me that the surroundings there were just what we needed. Nestled between the magnificent Sahyadri mountains, Igatpuri had much to offer—picturesque views, nature at its best, and ancient wisdom. Though it had extremes of climate—scorching summers, torrential monsoons, and extremely cold winters—the peace and stillness all around seemed just what the children needed. It even reminded me a little of Switzerland. After thinking about it for a while, I headed to the office and spoke to Gita Pai who manages the Sadhnalaya and conducts the most inspirational retreats there.

My sister Arnavaz introduced me to Gita in 1995, and she has always been a source of great inspiration to me. Gita called up Advocate S.B. Pawar, the lawyer who had undertaken all the legal formalities in setting up the Sadhnalaya. I was introduced to him that evening. After telling him what I was looking for, he took me the next evening to Awalkhed, my first visit there. "*Awal*," Advocate Pawar declared, "means 'No.1, the best' and '*khed*' is a village—hence Awalkhed is the 'No.1 best village!'" There was no proper road, only a dust track, and the rickshaw ride there was very bumpy. Awalkhed was about six kilometres away from the Sadhnalaya, but because of the bumpy ride, it took over half an hour to get there.

The bumpy ride to Awalkhed

We did not go to the land that Advocate Pawar had originally planned to show me, as the owner, an inhabitant of Igatpuri, was unavailable at the time. "See that land on top," he pointed to a hill in the distance, "that is the one I wanted to show you, but it is not possible today." A villager came along and spoke with Advocate Pawar. He turned to me and said, "See this piece of land? It is also very good." It was a plot adjacent to the one he had wanted to show me. We walked around this land for a while, but I was not convinced.

A few days later I visited the place again, this time with Binduben, who was visiting Igatpuri once again, her German friend Ursula Bhattacharjee, and Natasha Albuquerque, who was in charge of donor relations at Aseema at the time. It was evening and as we walked around, we saw the sun and moon at the same time. An enchanting sight! That night at Sadhnalaya I could not sleep. "Why was I doing this? The place was so remote, far from all things familiar to me, my family, my friends... I knew no one in Igatpuri... How would I run a residential school or for that matter any school there?"

The next morning Binduben was emphatic, "Too far and in the middle of nowhere, not at all suitable," she announced. So, I asked Advocate Pawar to show me other places closer to Sadhnalaya. However, most of the land in this area is tribal land that cannot be purchased. There is a law in India to safeguard the rights of the tribals, which prohibits the purchase of tribal land by a non-tribal.

We left Igatpuri asking Advocate Pawar to look for some other land for us. On a subsequent visit, he showed me a few other places, but there was always some issue, either it was tribal land, or there was some complication regarding ownership, or it was too small or too big! I could sense Advocate Pawar getting impatient with me. I kept asking him to show me the land which he had originally intended for us at Awalkhed, which he did not do. I would regularly call him from Mumbai to inquire if he had found something suitable and finally one day, he shouted, "The only land available is the one I showed you on the first day, there is no other land available," and slammed down the phone.

Now I was left to my own devices. I then started asking a few people I had met in Igatpuri if they could help us, but the truth is I did not know many people there. In the course of this search, I met Dina Simoes Guha.

A well-wisher of Aseema, Parvati Venkateswaran, who worked for the USIS Library in Mumbai, knew of my frequent visits to Igatpuri and she suggested I meet Dina. Dina had moved from Mumbai to Igatpuri about four years ago. She had, however, spent her childhood here. Her father was well known to the tribals, having often helped them when they had been cheated of their land. Dina later moved to the USA to complete her Master's in Education and became a teacher. She had also written many articles on education and was an extremely intelligent lady, passionate about her subject.

Armed with an address given to me by Parvati, Thrity Dolykuka, an Aseema volunteer, Ashok, Aseema's social worker, and I went one morning to meet Dina. She asked us to meet her at Simoes Wadi, a lovely open plot with many trees. Dina was planning to build her new home on this land. She was sitting there surrounded by her beloved dogs and seemed pleased to see us.

"Welcome to Igatpuri!" she greeted us. We exchanged pleasantries and briefly told her about Aseema. "We are considering starting a school," we said, "and are looking for a suitable plot of land." She seemed surprised and said, "When I returned to Igatpuri a few years ago, I was very keen to educate the local children, but they just don't seem to be interested." While she thought that starting a school was a good idea, she warned us about the authorities in Igatpuri, "A bunch of rascals," she said emphatically. "When I was growing up here, Igatpuri was inhabited by the British and Parsis and the place was full of beautiful rose gardens. Now, these rascals have turned the place into one big toilet," she added angrily. "I met the President of the Igatpuri Municipal Council the other day and told him to change the name of Igatpuri to 'Sandaspuri'!" (*sandas* is 'toilet' in Hindi). She warned us about the corruption and about the people who were exploiting the tribals and usurping their land.

As we were leaving, Dina mentioned, "I am going to Nashik tomorrow to meet the collector. Why don't you come with me?" Keen to know a little more about the region and the authorities, and thinking it would be an interesting outing, we readily agreed. The next day, our little party set out in my bright yellow Wagon R. It was our first visit to Nashik, a city much smaller than Mumbai. Once in the collector's office, Dina gave him a piece of her mind and told him all about the wrongdoings in Igatpuri. He seemed non-committal and not very interested in what she said. We left his office knowing that he was not inclined to interfere in the local affairs of Igatpuri, much less look into Dina's complaints. The visit to the collector was followed by a delicious thali lunch and a ride back to Igatpuri.

On the return journey, we brought up the subject of our land hunt once again. "You must meet Biharilal Chandak, a long-time resident of Igatpuri, and his son Punit. They may be able to help you."

Once in Igatpuri, we went to Biharilal's home. We met him on the portico of his old and sprawling bungalow. He was warm and friendly and happy to meet us. When we told him why we had come to Igatpuri, he was delighted.

Biharilal was in his late 70s. He was a strong, powerful, free-thinking man, interested in many things, but above all in education, agriculture, and spirituality. He believed that all the world was his family and honestly practised it. This belief had also rubbed off on his son Punit, whom we met later that evening. Punit ran the Bharat Radio Company, Bharat Petroleum's gas agency in Igatpuri.

More than anything else in the world, Biharilal wanted his children to have a good education, so in his younger days, he travelled around India to find a suitable school. Finally, he found one in Pondicherry— the Sri Aurobindo International Centre for Education (SAICE), which appealed to him very much. He also had a premonition that The Mother of Pondicherry may soon leave her body. So just weeks before Punit was to be born, he decided to move to Pondicherry with his family. The rest of the extended family in Igatpuri and Nashik protested and advised against this hurried decision, but Biharilal had made up his mind. He set out with his wife and four children in the third-class compartment of a train, in November 1973. A few days after they reached Pondicherry, Punit was born.

After a few years in that beautiful seaside city, Biharilal and his wife, Lakshmi, returned to Igatpuri, leaving their young children behind to continue schooling at SAICE. Biharilal was passionate about agriculture and organic farming and cultivated paddy in the fields in front of his home. He loved his cows as much as he loved his children and had many of the big variety of 'Dange' cows (a breed found in the region that gives little milk but of high quality). I think it was his dream that his children return to Igatpuri, educate the local children, and put into practice all that they had learnt in Pondicherry, and it thrilled him to hear that we, at Aseema, shared a similar vision.

Family of 'Dange' cows

"I would like to show you some land in Tringalwadi, a tribal village a few miles from Igatpuri," Biharilal suggested. "It is a remote tribal village and a perfect place for you to start your school. Dilbur, you can drive us all there tomorrow." Punit, being the more practical of the two, objected, "The road is steep and rough and it is very far. It will be impossible to go in a small car. I will arrange for a jeep."

The visit to Trigalwadi did not materialise then—it happened several years later in 2008 when we took the little children of the Anganwadi we would eventually build on a picnic, accompanied by Biharilal. It was a scenic place, but inaccessible and remote—a picturesque location for our school picnic, but certainly not for our school!

We often visited Biharilal and Punit. We needed all the help we could get in locating a suitable property for our school. In later years, after we purchased the property, Punit played an important role in setting up Aseema's education centre. He has his own particular way of functioning and can bulldoze you into taking action! His friend, Sandeep Sancheti, also played an important part in helping set up our Anganwadi and the pre-primary section of our education centre.

Punit is often suspicious of any new venture and it takes a while to convince him, but once this is done, there is no stopping him and he goes out of his way to assist you. The burden of running the gas agency, with all its difficulties, was getting to him and I think he would have loved to relocate to Pondicherry, where his sisters and brother continue to live. But his deep sense of responsibility to his family kept him in Igatpuri. Ever since he had started running the agency, and especially after the death of his mother in 2002, he worked long hours, 365 days a year. And in between a couple of arrest warrants, court cases and violence by political outfits, he attended to Aseema's work, ran errands for Dina and did all he could for many poor and vulnerable persons in Igatpuri. A rickshaw driver said to me the day after Punit's gas agency was terminated, "*Abhi Igatpuri ke garib log ko kaun dekhega?*" (Who will look after the poor people in Igatpuri now?)

16

The Igatpuri Project

"You do not have to be rich to be generous."

We continued to visit Igatpuri in the hope of finding a suitable property to set up an education centre. Meanwhile, in 2004, we were introduced to Dr Indra Munshi by Zarin D'Monte, our consultant child psychotherapist. Zarin had been volunteering at Aseema for several years, and when she heard of our visits to the tribal areas of Igatpuri she said, "Oh, you must meet Indra who has done so much work with the tribals. Her knowledge on the subject is immense and she will be able to guide you properly." Indra was head of the Department of Sociology at Mumbai University at the time. We met at her lovely and artistic home on Pali Hill.

Hospitable, warm and caring, she gave me a book she had written on 'Adivasis' (tribals) and shared her experiences at length. "I strongly suggest you do a study of the area to understand the needs of the people," she advised. "Yes, Dilbur, even if you are setting up a residential centre for some of your students from Mumbai, you must know about the local area you are going to work in. That is the first thing you should do. I can help you with the questions that need to be asked; we will make a simple questionnaire and you can conduct a survey there."

Another meeting was organised with her, attended by Thrity, Ashok, and Sonali Gonsalves, a student from the Nirmala Niketan College of Social Work, who volunteered with us at the time. Indra offered us tea and snacks, all exquisitely served. Then followed a detailed discussion on the objectives of setting up an education centre in this remote tribal area and how we should go about it.

After working on several drafts, the final questionnaire was ready, and we were good to go. She also gave us very practical advice on how to talk and interact with the tribals. She added a word of caution to me, "You, my dear, must be careful. Parsis have exploited the tribals of Dahanu for years and the tribals will initially be very suspicious of you."

Indra was right, but I'm not sure it had anything to do with the fact that I was a Parsi! It took many years for the tribals of Igatpuri to accept us. Initially, there was much scepticism. People from Mumbai usually came to grab their land. They could not believe that we only wanted to educate their children, without expecting anything in return.

Thrity, Ashok, and Sonali spent the next two weeks in Igatpuri visiting all the households in the main village of Awalkhed and the surrounding *wadis* (hamlets) of Karachiwadi, Jambulwadi, Rerewadi, Warachiwadi, Chandwadi, Phanaswadi, Jambhwadi, and Gowalwadi. They stayed at Sadhnalaya and would start immediately after breakfast, having packed a simple lunch. An autorickshaw driver had kindly agreed to take them daily to the main village. There was no proper road; it was more a mud track, full of stones, bumpy and backbreaking. From there, they would walk to each household, talking to the families and getting details about them—the number of members in the family, what they did, their education, the age of the children, and so on. Some of the friendlier people would invite them to lunch—and the simple fare would be shared by all.

I would call them every night, and they would tell me all that had happened. One night, they sounded sad. "In some of the villages, the people have nothing to eat. They sometimes have only one meal every two or three days. This includes the children," they said. We know about poverty in India, but we only expect to encounter it in the remotest villages of the poorest states of Bihar and Orissa. But to encounter such poverty in Igatpuri, which is only a three-hour drive from Mumbai, the financial capital of India! It was shocking and disheartening and the kind-hearted Thrity added, "I know our intention is to set up an education centre for some of our Mumbai children, but the children here need it more than ever. They really have nothing."

Once Thrity, Ashok, and Sonali were back in Mumbai, we met at Indra's home again and studied the data collected. There were many children who simply did not attend school. The reasons were many—the teacher is seldom at school, the children who do attend cannot even read or do simple maths, the children have to help on the farms and the older girls have to help with the housework, look after younger children or take the animals out to graze. When asked if they would send their children to school if something relevant and meaningful was taught, most parents answered in the affirmative.

We then decided to study the existing Anganwadis and schools in the area. There was a small Anganwadi in Phanaswadi, the village just behind Sadhnalaya. It catered to the children of three villages: Phanaswadi, Jambhwadi, and Gowalwadi.

Thrity, Ashok, and I visited this, and a few other Anganwadis and a couple of primary schools in some of the other villages. The few primary schools there only had classes till Grades 2 or 4. The condition in both the Anganwadis and schools was similarly dismal—a dingy, dark, dilapidated room, where a midday meal was cooked, in addition to providing education. The Anganwadi teacher had multiple duties— she had to maintain a record of all the births in the village, look after lactating mothers, be a part of the annual polio drives, ensure the polio vaccine was given to every child and be responsible for the midday meal. In addition to all that, the teacher also had to be responsible for the children's education and ensure they were learning. Quite a task!

Our pre-primary head at Aseema at the time was Nirmala Rao, and she suggested we ask Chitra Pancholi, a retired headmistress of a kindergarten school in Mumbai, to help us with the task of training the teachers. Chitra was willing, and we started an on-the-job training programme with four Anganwadi teachers in the wadis surrounding Igatpuri. We gave each of them a trunk full of education material and Chitra explained how it could be used when working with the little ones. For a couple of years, Thrity, and Chitra visited the Anganwadis every alternate month and spent a couple of days there monitoring their progress.

The dilapidated Anganwadi at Phanaswadi

The training was conducted in the Anganwadi at Phanaswadi, which was actually a room meant to be used as a *vyayamshala* (gymnasium). The teacher of that Anganwadi was a young woman named Sunita. She was the most enthusiastic of the teachers and Chitra was so pleased with her progress that she suggested, "It would be wonderful if Aseema could help set up a nicer environment for the children of this Anganwadi. I don't think the other three teachers are interested in learning anything new. They have made no progress with the children in their Anganwadis and often don't even attend my training." She went on to add, "Let us not waste time and energy and instead focus on one Anganwadi and make it better. The other teachers will see what is happening here and perhaps be motivated to replicate it in their villages."

We had discussions with the primary teacher of the adjoining school and with the local education officer. I have a very vivid recollection of the meeting with the education officer in Igatpuri town. It was the month of July, during the torrential monsoon in Igatpuri. Thrity, Chitra, and I had planned to ask him to allocate funds from the government budget to repair the Anganwadi, as it was in such a deplorable condition, with the roof leaking in many places. When we entered his office, we were shocked by what we saw—there sat the education officer at his desk, surrounded by buckets to collect the rainwater pouring down from holes in the roof! We were speechless! Rather than ask him for funding, we offered to repair the Anganwadi at our own cost! He happily agreed.

Unfortunately, there were complications. The room was 'officially' designated a gymnasium and not an Anganwadi, and we were not allowed to repair it. Meanwhile, the local government had issued a circular decreeing that the Anganwadi be shifted from the village of Phanaswadi to the adjoining village of Jambhwadi.

Once more, our little party headed for the office of the Education Officer. This time to ask, "Sir, since you have issued this circular, will you be providing a room to set up the Anganwadi in Jambhwadi? Or provide some land where a room can be built?" I politely added. This time he seemed irritated and said, "Yes, we have issued this circular. The Anganwadi can be conducted in the home of one of the villagers. Now please excuse me, I am busy and have a lot of important work to attend to."

We left his office dejected, but there was nothing further to be said or done. Sunita started her classes in the home of a villager. It worked for a while, but not for long. When the family had visitors, classes could not be conducted and finally, the children lost interest, attendance dwindled and Sunita spent most of her time simply rounding them up. Chitra and Thrity both announced, "Something has to be done urgently. Else, all our work of the past year will come to nought."

In the course of looking for land for our education centre, Ashok and I continued our regular visits to Jambhwadi. We asked the villagers if there was a room anyone would like to offer us on rent, or a vacant plot where we could build a room. It was a small village and nothing materialised.

One day, a tribal lady came up to us and said, "I see you have been coming to my village to educate our children. It makes me happy and I too want to do something." She pointed to a piece of land adjacent to where we stood. "See this? This is my land. I grow *'nachni'* and *'warai'* (local crops) here. It's for the use of my family. But I don't need all of this land and I would like to give you a part of it to set up the Anganwadi." This frail old lady was Sitabai Kavji Mengal, caring, compassionate, and generous. I was overwhelmed, and it took a while to comprehend all that she said.

The next day, she came with her son, Soma. She had brought with her some chalk and with her own hands, marked the beautiful red earth to indicate the part she would give us for the Anganwadi. "This is what I need," she pointed to where she would grow her *'nachni'* and *'warai'*, "and this is where you can build the Anganwadi." I realised then that she was not frail; she had strength that belied her frail form. She may not have been educated in the sense that we understand but she was far more enlightened, far more generous, and far more interested in educating the children of her village than so many people who pontificate about values and education and giving but do nothing. I did not know how to thank her and we simply held hands.

17

The Aseema Sitabai Kavji Mengal Anganwadi

"Not all of us can do great things. But we can do small things with great love."

– Mother Teresa

Punit introduced us to Sandeep Sancheti, an enthusiastic and hardworking young man who would help us construct the Anganwadi. Sandeep roped in his cousin, Sachin Sancheti, who was an engineer, to assist with the construction, and I requested my brother-in-law Hoshi Kapadia, who was an architect, to give me a simple plan for it. We loved what he gave and were all set to go!

The very important question of funding remained, so we approached the Mahindra & Mahindra factory in Igatpuri for help. It is located at the entrance of Igatpuri and the person in charge of their philanthropy was a young doctor, Dr Paul Bishwadeep. He showed great interest in our project and we received a donation from his company, which allowed us to do much of the work. The rest we raised from individual donors.

Dr Paul's wife studied architecture, and she helped whenever we needed any advice on construction. According to the plan, the Anganwadi was to have three classrooms. We couldn't afford the third, so we had two classrooms and a small storeroom between them. The third room remained a big open veranda in front of the school. Once built, the employees of Mahindra & Mahindra volunteered to paint the school and conduct a tree plantation drive.

The Anganwadi was inaugurated in June 2007 at the hands of Sitabai Kavji Mengal. It was a fulfilling moment for her as she performed the puja along with her son Soma. She had only one request that we employ Soma as a watchman. We employed both Soma and his wife, Sakrubai, Soma as watchman and Sakrubai as support staff to clean the school daily.

The children simply loved their new Anganwadi! It was airy, with a lot of light, beautiful surroundings, and a full view of the majestic Igatpuri mountains. The education material we had at the time was basic but well – designed and everything was neatly arranged on wooden shelves made by a local carpenter. The children sat on mats, as the rough floor would get very cold and damp during the monsoon. Thrity and Chitra were delighted with it all. Two new teachers joined us; one of them was Sonali Awhad. Sunita had to leave due to personal reasons, but the Anganwadi continues to do very well today under Durga Kamdi, a tribal residing in Phanaswadi.

There was no toilet attached to the Anganwadi initially for two reasons—the first was that the children were not used to having one in their homes, as open defecation was the norm. The second and main reason was that there was no money left to construct a toilet after the Anganwadi was built. It came many years later, together with a lovely play area in front of the school, complete with a see-saw and slide.

Sitabai Kavji Mengal inaugurating the new Anganwadi

A meal prepared by the Anganwadi helper was provided to the children daily. It was simple but nutritious and the children enjoyed it immensely. Soon after we started classes, Dr Paul organised a medical camp, not only for the children, but for their parents and the entire community as well, and the villagers turned out in large numbers to get themselves examined by the doctors.

Both Soma and Sakrubai worked at Aseema until they passed away in 2013. They were a devoted couple and very loyal to the organisation, helping beyond their call of duty. So fond was Soma of his beloved Sakrubai that he no longer wished to live after her death, and having consumed poison, passed away too. I remember their evening funeral, two small bodies laid out in the field with the magnificent Sahyadri range in the background, and could not help thanking God that Sitabai was no longer alive to witness this tragic sight.

Sitabai's grandchildren, who have received their entire education at Aseema from pre-primary to Grade 10, and some of the younger ones who continue to be in school, are aware that if it had not been for their grandmother, their lives would have been quite different. Her two grandsons, Ravi and Deepak, are now in college and are very proud of Sitabai. A nice photograph of her inaugurating the Anganwadi continues to adorn the walls of the Anganwadi.

18

The Family Goes to Igatpuri

The long search for land was coming to an end.

I usually share all the important events in my life with my brother, Sorab and my sister, Arnavaz and their families. While they have been a huge emotional support for all my initiatives, they think I work too much and sometimes take on more than I can handle. "You really need to slow down and get some rest" is something I frequently hear from Arnavaz. Sometimes it is more impatient, "Now you are overdoing it, stop it!"

In 2005, both of them, together with my sister-in-law Tannaz and brother-in-law Hoshi, accompanied me to Igatpuri. We spent three happy days at the retreat centre, enjoying the peace and quiet of the place. I took them to Awalkhed, to show them the very first piece of land that Advocate Pawar had pointed out to me.

As mentioned earlier, Advocate Pawar had been annoyed with me since I rejected the plots he had shown me, so Ashok, Thrity, and I continued our hunt independently. In some cases, we went as far as having the land surveyed, but for some reason or other, the deal never went through.

With every passing day, the search continued. But my mind kept going back to the first plot I had seen in the distance.

Advocate Pawar had promised to take me to it but never did.

An old friend, Purshottam Shenoy, then stepped in and made several trips to Igatpuri to try to get hold of that land for us. Finally, we had a breakthrough, and he was able to convince the owners to let us see it. The plot was large, much larger than I had imagined. It spread across hills and valleys; it was a stone's throw from the main village of Awalkhed, surrounded by little hamlets with Igatpuri's solid mountains in the distance. It was beautiful and love at first sight! "This is it," I remember saying to myself, "this is what we need. God, please help us get this land."

The land at Awalkhed

Soon thereafter, I brought Sorab and Arnavaz to see it and to meet the owners. Initially, I think they were taken aback; the bumpy ride and the remoteness of the place were crucial factors to consider. But they, too, loved the landscape, the greenery, and the stillness of the place. It was the month of March and the sun beat down on us. While Arnavaz, Hoshi, and I walked around the land, Sorab and Tannaz sat under a shady tree nearby. They were met by Bhagubai Pawar, a villager, who went up to them and cheerfully said, "Namaste, what are you doing here?" Friendly by nature, she was curious about us.

When Sorab told her why we were there, she sprang into action. "Come, I will show you around," she announced. She and her husband, Sadu, joined us on our walk around the land. They knew exactly where it began and ended and pointed to trees and stones to show us the extent of the property, a bit confusing to us but making complete sense to them, "Look, the property starts here and ends there."

Arnavaz leaned over and whispered, "Bhagubai will be Aseema's Shobha in Igatpuri." We laughed, not knowing at the time how true that would be. Shobha had joined us when we started our work in Mumbai. She has been a great help to us for more than 15 years and still keeps in touch.

The owners of the land, Vinayak Vaze and Ajay Lunavat, finally arrived and showed us around. There was one big plateau where we could build the school and two smaller plateaus on either side, separated by two deep valleys. "Ideal for water harvesting," I thought to myself, "in this place that has such a water shortage." After a few hours spent on the land, getting to know the owners better and asking them to share all the necessary documents and land records, we departed.

It seemed like the long search for land had finally come to an end. But little did I realise that this was only the beginning. What a long and winding road lay ahead until we could finally set up our school!

19

Gratitude and the Quest for Water

"For a web begun, God sends thread."

– Proverb

Purshottam now had the task of gathering all the land documents and showing them to a lawyer. After making inquiries in Igatpuri he learnt that the best person for the job was Advocate Pawar, as he had a great deal of experience in land matters. We knew we had to be cautious, for the same piece of land is often sold to several different parties! We had to make sure that the title to the land was clear. Our funding was minimal; we could not risk losing a single paisa. And so, it was back to Advocate Pawar. "I am not sure he will take up our matter," I warned Purshottam. "He was furious with me the last time we spoke." But Advocate Pawar bore no grudge and seemed happy to help us.

"Well, madam," he announced, "you are finally buying the Awalkhed land. It is a very good thing. Don't worry, I will make sure that everything is alright." From that moment on, he provided full support and often visits our school when there is a function.

Finally, in mid-2006, after what felt like an endless search, the much-longed-for land became Aseema's. Thrity came with me to the registrar's office, and immediately after the registration, we went to the Paramahansa Yogananda Sadhnalaya. We were getting late to catch our train back to Mumbai, but there was no way I could leave before going to the wishing well and offering my heartfelt gratitude. Getting the land had taken almost two-and-a-half years. It had not been easy for me and my two faithful companions during this time— Thrity and Ashok. Thrity was nearly 70 years old but had the spirit of a 17-year-old, and Ashok undertook all the hard tasks like spending hours in the hot summer months searching for land and overseeing land surveys. I would not have been able to do this without their help and support.

Our next task was to plan what kind of education centre we would set up and to look for donors interested in supporting us. In December 2006, Mr Vasa, a businessman in Mumbai who had been supporting our work at the Pali Chimbai Municipal School, expressed interest in visiting Igatpuri. His wife had recently passed away, and he wanted to do something in her memory. Ashok and I went with Mr Vasa in his car to Awalkhed.

After a long, bumpy ride, we reached our site. It had not been fenced yet, and we had no gate, as all our money at the time had been used to procure the land. We got out of the car and walked to our property. The entrance was rough and uneven, but Ashok was so used to it that he raced ahead. I helped Mr Vasa but he, unfortunately, tripped and fell. "Where have you brought me?" he thundered, "There is no road, no water, no nothing here!" he went on, "Let us go back, please." There was nothing we could do to convince him to stay. Mr Vasa was not interested in seeing our beautiful valleys and plateaus and trees, so we quietly and sadly got into the car and headed back. We guessed there was no hope of Mr Vasa helping us with this project and we were right.

We knew we had to do something to get water. So, we contacted Aajay Rao, a horticulturist, who had also studied landscaping and water harvesting. He visited us and suggested a spot where we could dig a well. This location was confirmed, and we started the blasting work. Igatpuri receives a great deal of rainfall every year. During the monsoon months, from June to September, we rarely see the sun, and the humidity is so high that even a handkerchief takes more than ten days to dry. Despite the heavy monsoon, there is an acute shortage of water from March onwards, till the next monsoon. We realised that the first thing we needed to do was to be self-sufficient in water.

Women trudge up the steep slope from the wells below to their homes on top

There was no municipal pipeline supplying water to Awalkhed and the *wadis*. The village of Awalkhed has two wells located at the bottom of the steep slope that leads to the village. In summer, they too would dry up and had to be filled with water brought by tankers from Igatpuri town. There is no water source in the main village. From December onwards, the women trudge up the steep slope from the wells below to their homes on top twice a day simply to meet their daily needs. While they balance the numerous pots on their head beautifully, it is an exhausting and time-consuming task. In the early years, when they had learnt that Aseema was going to build a school for their children, one of the women asked, "Why don't you do something to help us get water?"

We had felt helpless at the time and hoped that on a future date, we would be able to help them with this too. However, I often had to remind myself that we would not be able to solve every issue that cropped up. Our work was to provide education and ensure that we did a good job of it.

Meanwhile, work on the well was proceeding at the spot Aajay Rao had identified, and we blasted till a stream opened up and showed signs of filling the well. While we did manage to strike water, this well only has enough to last until March. After March, the water table is so low that we have to depend on other sources. Many years later, we dug another well, but that is a story for another chapter.

20

The Papier Mâché Goat

"Every step taken in mindfulness brings us one step closer to healing ourselves and the planet."

– Thich Nhat Hanh

During the monsoon of 2007, volunteers from Mahindra & Mahindra undertook a tree plantation drive and planted more than 600 trees, mainly acacia, and gulmohar on our land. It was only years later that we learnt that it is best to plant only local, indigenous trees; acacia and gulmohar are not indigenous species. While not all survived, some did, but our land is so rocky that they have taken many years to grow and flower.

We also had students from the prestigious Tata Institute of Social Sciences (TISS) do an internship in Igatpuri and update the data that Thrity, Ashok, and Sonali had collected a couple of years ago. I remember the interns, Sukruti and Donald, being horrified when they saw what was happening at one Anganwadi.

"Ma'am please look at this. What they have cooked has gone bad, but they were going to feed it to the children anyway." They held up a thin plastic bag that contained what looked like a messy porridge. "We pleaded with the teacher not to give it to the children, and she finally realised it was bad and threw it away."

We appointed Bhagubai to look after our property during the day, and her son, along with another boy from the village, served as night watchmen. The two boys ended up having a big fight and quit. Now we had only Bhagubai and a tribal lady, Atiyabai, who doubled as security staff and gardeners.

Punit and Sandeep both kept an eye on the property too. They assisted with the well, helped with the tree plantation, and finally, when we could afford it, fenced the property as well. A proper access road to the property was also built to avoid another incident like we had with poor Mr Vasa!

I was in Mumbai when I got a call from Sandeep in early 2008. "Madam, we have a problem. A man has committed suicide on our land."

This was shocking news, and I immediately replied, "How did that happen and who is he?" "We don't know exactly; the body has just been found and the police are expected soon," he said. "Don't worry, I will come immediately," I replied. I was very upset and wanted to leave for Igatpuri right away. "No, don't come now. We will handle the matter and let you know when you are needed," said Sandeep.

I was restless and shared this news with Joan Manohar, a senior and respected colleague. "Wait till you get further news from Punit and Sandeep," she advised, "but you must go and say some prayers at the site. You don't need a priest. Just recite your Parsi prayers."

I soon left for Igatpuri, and on the way there, informed my sister Arnavaz what had happened. She was as concerned as I was and spoke to our dear friend Lalita Krishnan, who was one of the most spiritual and godly people we knew.

Lalita told Arnavaz, "Please tell Dilbur not to worry, but do ask her to go to the spot where this has happened and chant the *Hanuman Chalisa*." For all Hindus, *Hanuman Chalisa* is a very powerful prayer. It praises the strength, wisdom, and knowledge of Hanuman, the Hindu monkey God, and calls upon Him to remove all difficulties and invoke His blessings on the devotee.

Arnavaz, not wanting me to be alone, left Pune, where she lived, for Igatpuri. When she arrived, she told me what Lalita had asked us to do.

"But I don't know the *Hanuman Chalisa*," I said, "and neither do you!" So, we called Punit, who brought us prayer books of the chant.

The reason both Joan and Lalita wanted us to pray was because here we were, about to start an important project, perhaps Aseema's most important project to date, and this inauspicious incident had happened at our site. We had no idea at the time whether any complications or legal issues would arise because of the incident. Prayers would surely help, they felt, and so did we.

Nirmala Rao, our pre-primary head in Mumbai, used to visit Igatpuri once a month to see how the children were progressing, and she happened to be in Igatpuri when Arnavaz arrived from Pune. We shared what had happened with her and told her that we would be going to Awalkhed the next day to chant the *Hanuman Chalisa*, "Which incidentally neither of us knows". She immediately said, "Oh, I know the prayer; I chant it often. I will come with you tomorrow after my class. Let us also take some *agarbattis* (incense sticks) with us," she added. We were enormously relieved.

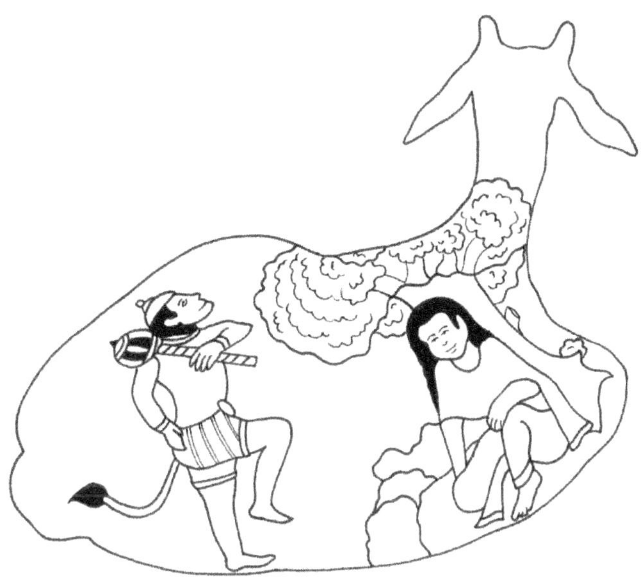

The Papier Mâché Goat

The next day, the three of us went to the spot. It was in one of the valleys under an *umber* (wild fig) tree. We sat and prayed and Nirmala chanted the *Hanuman Chalisa* and we lit the *agarbattis*. It gave us much relief and provided closure to the whole incident.

We learnt later from the police that the man was from a village near Delhi. He had been murdered and subsequently brought there. It was only made to appear like he had hanged himself. We would never know the whole story, but we were glad we performed our little prayer ceremony to put the unpleasant incident behind us, and for the soul of the poor deceased.

That evening, Nirmala and I left for Mumbai. When I arrived home, there was a big box in my living room with 'Happy Birthday' written on it. On opening it, I found a marvellous papier mâché goat made by an Aseema alumnus, Ramesh Ghayal. He was a very talented boy who had been trained by Varsha. "I have to show Ramesh an object only once, and he gives me something ten times better," Varsha frequently said of him.

I often received very sweet birthday and other greeting cards from the children but this was a complete surprise! I carefully lifted the goat out of the box and admired the art Ramesh had done on it. As I turned it around, I was dumbfounded. Ramesh had painted a magnificent Hanuman on one side of the goat.

My thoughts reeled at all that had happened the past few days. We had not shared the sad news of the man's death with anyone, and the only people who knew about it were Joan, Nirmala, Arnavaz, Sandeep, Punit, and me. What made Ramesh paint Hanuman on the goat? I have no idea, but I liked to think it symbolised that this present difficulty was conclusively over. It probably was, as we heard no more about the case from either the police or anyone else.

The concept of oneness, or the belief that everything in the universe is part of the same fundamental whole, exists in many cultures and philosophical, religious, spiritual, and scientific traditions. It can also be backed by some quantum theories. Despite seeming like people and events are far removed from one another, the same basic essence permeates everything. The Hanuman chant could have nothing to do with the papier mâché goat, but it might just be that events extend beyond the individual to encompass wider aspects of humankind, life, nature, and even the cosmos.

The goat with Hanuman on it still holds a place of pride in my living room.

21

Experiments with Rammed Earth and Bamboo

If we will be quiet and ready enough, we shall find compensation in every disappointment.

– Henry David Thoreau

Before us lay the task of finding an architect who would design and build the school. We initiated discussions with a few architects and even got one from Pondicherry to submit a plan. But it was not what we had imagined and thought it would be far more practical to work with someone closer to Igatpuri. We then approached a young architect who was about to start an independent practice; he suggested we go in for a rammed-earth construction with bamboo rafters. We experimented with a single classroom and a bathroom but it was nothing short of a disaster!

Sitting in a small room at the entrance of the property, we watched the rammed-earth experiment unfold. We witnessed the entire exercise, which happened in April and May 2009, with much trepidation and anxiety. We were grateful, however, to be sheltered from the hot sun, as there was not a single tree on the main plateau at the time. Progress was slow and it soon became obvious that the contractor from Nashik did not know how to handle the rammed earth and bamboo construction.

Watching the construction from the small room at the entrance

After the bathroom was completed, we abandoned the idea of rammed earth for the classroom and decided to opt for a conventional room made with bricks.

This taught me an important lesson. If one is going to try out something different and experimental, in this case, a rammed-earth construction in an area like Igatpuri with heavy rainfall, and where the local labour does not know the technique, then one should stay onsite and on the job at all times to ensure the task is well executed. It cannot be done long distance.

To make matters worse, one night I was stung by a scorpion on my finger. We were staying at the retreat centre at the time and it happened as I was drawing the curtains. At the first prick, I thought someone had left a needle in the new curtains. Then, when the pain became excruciating, I looked into the folds of the curtain and saw a big black scorpion. It was frightening! I ran out of my room and called my companions. "I think I have been stung by a scorpion," I cried.

I was very scared and not sure what would happen next. Ashok, the architect, and Ravi Kundalia, the son of close friends, were with me at the time. No one knew exactly what was to be done. "Aunty, please keep your arm up," advised young Ravi. "I think we should tie your forearm with a tight tourniquet," said the architect. Ashok was determined to find the scorpion. He went into my room, brought it out, showed it to everyone proudly, and then killed it. Punit was in Pondicherry at the time, so I called Sandeep, who immediately made an appointment with a doctor in the town.

It was almost 9:00 p.m., but the doctor's clinic was packed. Seeing the deathly look on my face, none of the waiting patients objected to my going directly into the doctor's cabin with Sandeep. The doctor attended to me immediately, "Tell me, where has the scorpion stung you?" "Here," I whispered, showing him my now swollen finger. I was barely audible, so severe was the pain by then. "I am giving you an injection," he said. Three injections were given, and the pain subsided almost instantly. "You will have to take these medicines for five days," he said, writing out a prescription. Feeling slightly better, I ventured to ask, "Is this dangerous, doctor? Will I be ok?" His reply was not entirely comforting, "There are complications occasionally. I am giving you my cell phone number. If you have any problem tonight, please call me immediately." Seeing the look on my face, he quickly added, "But complications happen rarely, don't worry." Slightly relieved, we left his clinic. To cheer us all up, we had dinner at Manas Hotel and then proceeded to the retreat centre.

"I am afraid to sleep in the same room," I meekly said once we were back. "Aunty, don't worry," were Ravi's encouraging words, "it is not likely that another scorpion will sting you tonight; that would be too much!"

I couldn't help smiling and went to bed. Mercifully, I slept soundly and except for the swelling on my hand, which took many days to subside, everything was soon perfectly well.

A few days later, Raghu Rai came to Igatpuri. He was an engineer who had studied at IIT and was experienced in environmental issues. He had been sent by Ravi's parents to help us with water harvesting. Raghu worked tirelessly for more than a week surveying the hillsides and marking where contour trenches should be located, with Ravi enthusiastically helping him. Raghu also suggested where check dams should be located in both valleys.

Joan Manohar, our COO at the time, and Indra visited during this time and both were happy to see the property, but were appalled by the construction. Both warned, "You must do something quickly to stop this rammed-earth experiment." But the monsoon was just around the corner, and the roof had to go up before we could stop it.

It finally went up two days before the monsoon set in. But the problems with the construction team took much longer to solve and ended with much disagreement and disappointment on all sides.

22

The Anganwadi Grows to Grade 1

*The children were happy and confident and enjoyed
coming to school.*

Settling on a construction team and attending to several other matters took almost a year. During that year, much had taken place. The children had started coming to the Sitabai Kavji Mengal Anganwadi regularly. Chitra and the teachers were happy with their progress, and some of them were ready to be promoted to Grade 1.

We approached the primary school headmaster in Phanaswadi and requested him: "Can we admit some of our children to your school, please?" We knew that the headmaster had a host of other duties and was not able to attend school daily. We also knew that he had four classes in his school, from Grades 1 to 4, and as he was the only teacher there, it was impossible for him to give all the children equal attention. The children who had studied at our Anganwadi for more than two years were fully ready for Grade 1 and we did not want their learning to be compromised. So, we suggested, "We will keep the children in our Anganwadi and our teachers will continue to teach them. We request you to let them appear for the final exam from your school."

We thought this would be a win-win situation for all. Our teachers would make sure the children were progressing well in their studies, and the children could appear for their examinations through the school. The headmaster seemed to like the idea and suggested we meet the education officer in Igatpuri to discuss the matter further, which we did.

"I will come and visit your school with my team," said the education officer. "I need to see what you are doing."

A couple of weeks later, he visited us with two other officers. "Yes, I like your school very much," he announced. "The children are learning well. And the material you have is good. But this is an important decision and I will need to discuss it with my seniors."

Weeks later, we finally received a letter from him stating that our proposal had not been accepted. Unofficially, we also received a message saying that if some "compensation" was awarded, we may be allowed to enrol children in the school at Phanaswadi.

It was very discouraging, but by then we were used to how things functioned. At the time, Aseema had been working for almost 10 years, and because we lived by our principles, we knew that delays and even refusals would come our way. Now, this particular education officer was to retire a few weeks later, but we read an article that appeared in all the local newspapers stating that he had been suspended at the retirement ceremony itself, on charges of corruption.

Our Social Worker at a tribal home

Incidents such as these made us realise that the sooner we had our own school, the better. Finding the right construction team, putting together proposals for funding and getting people interested in the project now became a priority. Most of our donors were from Mumbai, who were initially not inclined to donate to causes in faraway Igatpuri, but we were convinced we had to find a way.

Once we started Grade 1 classes, two new teachers joined us—Baban Kadam and Charulata Chavan. As it was the start of the academic year, more children were admitted to the Anganwadi. The very little ones would wail when their mothers left and sometimes the villagers couldn't understand why we were admitting children as young as two-and-a-half and three years to a school.

Baban, Charulata, and Sonali continue to work at Aseema till date. Baban is now our social worker, while Charulata works with pre-primary children and has been trained in the Montessori approach. Sonali, who joined us when she was only 17, has completed her Bachelor in Education (B.Ed.) and now teaches the secondary section.

The children enjoyed coming to the Sitabai Kavji Mengal Anganwadi, and because the environment was so pleasant and conducive to learning, they thrived. A simple meal would be given to them at noon and they continued to have entertaining annual and sports days. Those invited as chief guests on these occasions always remarked, "The children seem so very happy and confident. They really do enjoy coming to school."

Picnics were held at nearby locations, and the older children enjoyed them. The little ones would be fast asleep by the time we arrived at the picnic spot, so unused were they to any kind of travel. Some special snacks and a sweet were always served at picnics. When asked if they would like anything more, a little boy, Parshuram, would always say, "Yes, one more *gulab jamun* (a popular Indian sweet) please." He often ended up eating almost seven to eight of those delicious sweets and nothing else, but on those special days, it was very hard for us to say no to him.

Patiently waiting for the lights to come on

On all our visits to Igatpuri, which took place almost every month, we continued to stay at the retreat centre, which was close to the Anganwadi. Sometimes, when a retreat was in session, we stayed at another retreat centre in the town. We were very fortunate that they allowed us to do so because both centres had very strict rules. Igatpuri did not have many hotels, and at that time we could not afford one in any case.

Electricity in Igatpuri has always been a problem and on many days, there was no electricity at all. Living in Mumbai, we have no such problem, so it was difficult to get used to this. After working all day, returning to a dark room was depressing. It was very hot in summer without a fan, so Thrity, Ashok, and I would sit on the steps of the main building and wait patiently. When the lights came on, our mood would lift and we immediately felt infinitely better! I realised then how much these little comforts of life that we take so much for granted, affect our well-being and outlook.

In the monsoon came another problem to which I was never accustomed. Owing to the extreme humidity, everything felt damp—the mattress, the towels, and even one's clothes. It was not possible to wash any clothes at this time as nothing would dry. Even a thin handkerchief would take more than 10 days to dry! On windy days, you could feel the chilly, humid air creeping into your bones. The only thing that kept me comfortable was applying a soothing Ayurvedic balm all over my body before getting into bed. When I asked a local resident how they managed to dry their clothes during the monsoon, she simply said, "Oh, we hang everything in our kitchen and it dries in the heat generated by the stove." Well, the retreat centre kitchen was certainly not available for this purpose, so all we could do was carry extra clothes!

But we survived through it all and I think made us stronger, more tolerant, and more resilient.

23

Unexpected News

"You can fool all the people some of the time, and some of the people all the time, but you cannot fool all the people all the time."

When we were in Igatpuri during the summer months, Thrity and I would go to the well on our school site every morning at 6:00 a.m. The local women came there to draw water as it was closer to them than the village well, and also because, occasionally, there was no water in the village well. This helped us get to know them better. At this time, we did not need the water as our school had not yet been built, and we were more than happy to make life easier for the women. I had always hoped that one day, both the village and the school would be self-sufficient in water. But for the moment, our focus remained on building the school and providing quality education.

After one such morning visit to the well, we had some errands to run in Igatpuri so we drove in my yellow Wagon R to town, some nine kilometres away. The villagers had started calling it "Madam's yellow taxi", just as ten years ago in Mumbai, the children, and community referred to the second-hand Maruti 800 I had at the time, as "Teacher's blue taxi".

Thrity and I drove past the Vipassana meditation centre and turned towards the lane leading to Ram Mandir and the market. A brand-new garbage van was blocking the narrow street collecting garbage. As we waited behind it, Thrity piped up, "Dilbur, I would like to see how they are segregating the garbage." Aware of Thrity's keen interest in garbage collection and separation, I replied, "Sure, go ahead." She was very particular about waste management and cleanliness and often told me,

"People talk about beautification, but if they simply kept things clean, things will automatically look beautiful." I couldn't have agreed more!

While she got out of the car and observed what they were doing, I was getting restless waiting in the heat, so I got out as well and chatted with one of the sanitation workers, "Will your new van also come to Awalkhed to collect the garbage?" I casually asked. His reply came as a shock. "Yes, we are planning to come to Awalkhed to dump this garbage." Not believing my ears, I asked again, "You are going to dump Igatpuri's garbage in Awalkhed?" Pat came the reply, "Yes, the municipal council is purchasing land in Awalkhed so that all of Igatpuri's garbage can be thrown there."

The garbage van moved on; Thrity and I hurriedly got into the car and continued our journey. "I don't understand why people don't do their work properly," Thrity said, irritated. "Such a nice van with separate compartments for wet and dry garbage, but everything is just dumped all together. I don't know when things in our country will improve." Even as I listened to her, my mind was on what I had just been told by the sanitation worker, and I shared it with her. She was shocked and said, "We will have to look into it or they will make a mess of everything."

The first rains in Awalkhed

We finished our work in the town and returned to the retreat centre. All the while, my thoughts kept going back to what the sanitation worker had told me, and I decided to call the president of the municipal council, Sanjay Indulkar, to whom Advocate Pawar had introduced me.

Pleasantries over, I got straight to the point, "I heard today that the Igatpuri Municipal Council is proposing to dump the town's garbage at Awalkhed, is that right?"

After a moment's silence, he replied, "No, I have not heard anything about this proposal." I was slightly relieved, but knew we had to get to the bottom of it.

The first rains arrived and thundered all over Igatpuri. Many village homes, simple mud structures, were completely destroyed with their roofs blown off. Wanton destruction on one hand and relief on the other, as the heat had become oppressive and the farmers desperately needed water for their crops. Once the monsoon sets in, the whole of Awalkhed and the surrounding hamlets are covered in clouds every evening, which lift only the following morning. In a matter of days, the parched red-brown earth vanishes and a carpet of green appears everywhere. All is lush and soothing to the eyes.

Awalkhed and the surrounding villages are catchment areas. Numerous rivers have their source here and connect with the Bhima River which ultimately leads to the important Vaitarna Project that supplies water to Mumbai city. The rough road from Phanaswadi to Awalkhed was submerged at several low points during the torrential monsoon. A few years ago, a number of buffaloes were washed away near the Zoiti River, which is just outside Awalkhed village, because the current was so strong. A local teacher was rescued by the villagers just in time, or she too would have met the same fate as the buffaloes.

When I asked Bhagubai if she had heard of the Igatpuri Municipal Council's proposal to buy land in Awalkhed to dump their garbage, she first said it was impossible. "Why should they bring their rubbish and dump it on us?" she questioned angrily. "We don't throw our rubbish in Igatpuri." But it made her start thinking and finally, she said, "Don't worry, I'll look into it." A couple of weeks later, she told me that she knew a sanitation officer who worked in the municipal council. "Let us go to meet him to find out what they are planning," she suggested, and added, "but we will have to be careful."

So, one evening, we arrived at the lovely little cottage of the sanitation officer. As we admired the plants in his garden, he came out to greet us, "Do come in and have a cup of coffee." He was hospitable and friendly. "When you leave, I will give you some cuttings. Just tell me which plants you like." Over coffee and biscuits, he was forthcoming and said, "Yes, the deal to purchase the land is almost finalised and soon we will take all the waste from Igatpuri and deposit it on this land." He even named the villager who had agreed to sell the land to the municipal council.

On hearing this, we could barely swallow our coffee and soon took our leave, but not before Bhagubai took the plant cuttings. "Do visit again," said the kindly officer, "and let me know if you would like any more plants."

We were quiet until we settled down in the car and drove away. "See, I told you we would find out everything," Bhagubai announced triumphantly. "He has given us all the news."

"But," I ventured, "Sanjay Indulkar, who is the president of the municipal council, clearly told me that there was no such plan." By that time, Bhagubai was livid. "You don't know that man. I do, we all do." She went on, "Madam, these are politicians. They don't always speak the truth. They will only serve their own interests." Wise words from this lady who had no formal education. Besides having learnt to write her name, she could neither read nor write. "I told you we will find out the truth..." she went on, and before I could add, "and the truth will set us free," Bhagubai continued, "no harm ever comes to those who speak the truth. Madam, I always speak the truth. Don't you worry, we will find a way out of this problem."

When I shared the news with Punit and Sandeep, Punit simply said, "We will see that this does not happen. I have my ways." But I was worried, very worried, when Bhagubai and Sandeep found out that the land the municipal council was to purchase was a tract belonging to a tribal lady called Laxmibai Warghade. This property was right next to the two village wells that were the only source of water, including drinking water, for the villagers, and also very close to our own well. It was adjoining the Zoiti River, which flowed into the Bhima and ultimately the Vailtarna River. Was the municipal council going to dump the garbage from the Igatpuri town on this land? Where had this insane idea originated? And who was responsible for it?

The thought that was uppermost in my mind at the time was that there was so much evil in this world, one simply couldn't run away from it. The only way was to oppose it and do everything in one's power to see that good prevailed and justice was done.

24

The Battle

"The world will not be destroyed by those who do evil, but by those who watch them without doing anything."

– Albert Einstein

We decided to take Advocate Pawar's advice. His first reaction was, "They have gone mad! This is not the place to have a garbage depot. It lies to the west of Igatpuri town. And most important of all, it is a catchment area and the rivers from here connect with the Middle Vaitarna." He added, "Let the villagers know this is happening. They cannot do this without the *tharao* (resolution) of the Gram Sabha. It is illegal." An appeal was prepared that Bhagubai shared with the villagers, and hundreds of signatures were obtained overnight. The villagers had no idea of what was happening and had no knowledge of the project.

Land adjoining the Zoiti River

The only exception was one man—the *Sarpanch*, the head of the village, Baban Kewari. His signature had been taken when he was intoxicated, in a letter that stated he had no objection to the project. No one in the entire village knew about the plan to dump Igatpuri's waste in Awalkhed. The lady Warghade, who sold her land to the municipal council, claimed she had been told by them that they would build bungalows on the property and that her son was promised a job as a watchman. It appears that Mrs Warghade was heavily in debt and, being under tremendous pressure to repay the debt, had agreed to sell her land.

The appeal signed by all the villagers was submitted to the collector in Nashik by the Sarpanch and by two other senior and respected villagers in July 2008. The villagers had set out the facts and opposed the setting up of the garbage depot at Awalkhed. The collector simply said that he would look into the matter.

We also met Sanjay Indulkar, the president of Igatpuri Municipal Council, who said, "A high-level government committee has selected this site over five other sites, but if there is a threat to the environment, I will be willing to come with you to the collector." We then met the Divisional Commissioner in Nashik who said that he would study the environmental effects of the proposed project.

We decided to get an expert opinion on the matter and appointed an agency to undertake an environmental assessment. Their team visited the Awalkhed site, and several other sites, and drew up a detailed report clearly stating that there would be a negative impact on the environment and that the risk of leachate contamination of the wells and river nearby was very high. They also pointed out that the municipal solid waste management rules would be violated if the project was set up at the Awalkhed site and suggested a couple of other sites more suitable for this project.

We shared this report with all the concerned officers and authorities in Igatpuri and in Nashik. How the Maharashtra Pollution Control

Board (MPCB) and the Ground Water Authority had both given their no-objection certificates to go ahead with the site at Awalkhed was a mystery.

In early May 2009, a committee consisting of very senior officials from various government departments, including, the MPCB, Ground Water Authority, the Tehsildar of Igatpuri, and the chief officer of the municipal council visited the Awalkhed site and also the other suggested sites.

The committee presented a report to the Divisional Commissioner, who was convinced about the environmental damage that would be caused. He then passed an order that clearly stated that the site at Awalkhed was not suitable and directed that it be shifted to another location.

This was a huge relief. After a year of running from pillar to post, visiting every concerned government official, looking for alternative sites ourselves, and facing hostility from the municipal council officers, finally, there was light at the end of the tunnel. Now we could go back to our work and focus on education and building our school. So much remained to be done, and we were happy to get on with our main task.

A year later, on May 5, 2010, a new divisional commissioner, without giving us any notice, passed an order that completely reversed the order of his predecessor. It arrived at our Mumbai office by registered post and we were shocked! Our visits to the office of the Divisional Commissioner in Nashik resumed and also to all the other government offices in Nashik, Igatpuri, and the Mantralaya (the headquarters of the Maharashtra Government) in Mumbai.

Ultimately, we were left with no choice but to file a writ petition in the Bombay High Court challenging the order of the new divisional commissioner regarding setting up this project at Awalkhed. The villagers, too, filed a similar petition. Today, 13 years later, the matter is still in the court but a stay order is in force which prevents the Igatpuri Municipal Council from starting its ill-conceived project at Awalkhed.

The help that senior lawyers Rafiq Dada and Percy Ghandy (now deceased) have given us has been invaluable. The solicitor's firm of Maneksha & Sethna, and in particular Advocate Shezad Najamessani, stood by us throughout and helped with all the legal paperwork and formalities. Senior lawyers Fredun DeVitre, Darius Khambatta and Milind Sathe briefed by Solicitor Nilesh Modi of Rustomji & Ginwala took on the case of the villagers and assisted them through this difficult time. Advice from Fali Nariman, India's top jurist, when we went to the Supreme Court was invaluable and the thoroughness with which he examined our case was a true learning experience. "No getting emotional," he shouted at me at one conference, "that's the problem with all you NGO chaps. If we are to win the case, we have to be practical, stick to the facts, and do every bit of homework." And he made sure we did!

All this taught me an important lesson. Though the tribals, the poor, and the downtrodden have no voice at most times, they too, with support, can make their voices heard. There are good, noble people everywhere and we have to call upon the universe to help us reach out to them. The fight against evil and the struggle, no matter how exhausting, for purity and good in this world, has to go on. As Bhagubai expressed, "It is only the truth that will set us free."

25

The Pre-Primary School at Awalkhed

"I know the price of success: dedication, hard work, and an unremitting devotion to the things you want to see happen."

– Frank Lloyd Wright

We had now raised a certain amount of funding and were ready to start construction of our pre-primary school on our own land at Awalkhed. We appointed a young architect, Khushru Irani, and this time an experienced contractor from Igatpuri, Tinu Verma. Sandeep and Sachin Sancheti supervised the day-to-day work.

Many little children from Awalkhed and the surrounding *wadis* enrolled, and we used the classroom that we had built previously to accommodate them and appointed Durga Kamdi as their teacher. Baban Kadam joined Durga to teach these children. It was sometimes a challenge getting all the children to attend, especially during the monsoon, when they would often accompany their parents to the fields to help with sowing. Another problem was that the older girls were often not sent to school, as they were made to look after the very little children at home and do all the housework. They also spent much of their time grazing their cattle. Baban and Durga made frequent visits to the children's homes to explain the importance of education to the parents. This was, however, a slow process.

Sandeep and Sachin put up a temporary structure behind the classroom which served as a kitchen and we started preparing the midday meal there—very simple, but wholesome, and nutritious.

Construction of the main pre-primary school took a year and a half and we inaugurated the building on March 23, 2011. The function went on for two days. There were many people to invite. The first day was reserved for the local tribal community who attended in large numbers. The Sarpanch, the Deputy Sarpanch, and the Police Patil were felicitated on this day.

On the second day, all the parents of our students attended. Punctuality is not the strong point of many Indians. We had asked the parents to be present at 10:00 a.m. knowing that they would slowly make their way to school any time between 10:00 a.m. and 12:00 noon! At 10:00 a.m. there were few who had assembled, so we started playing the music at full volume on the loudspeaker so that it was audible in all the surrounding areas. Hearing the lively and welcoming music, the parents came walking from their hamlets toward the music and to the school.

The chief guest was Chaitram Pawar, a tribal who had done some amazing community work in the village of Baripada in Maharashtra. Meenaz and Moe Kassam were the guests of honour. They have been ardent supporters of our work and generous donors. Meenaz is also on Aseema's Board of Advisors. All our donors and well-wishers who had supported this project attended the inauguration. Carol Donoughue, trustee of the Vidya Trust and a long-time supporter of Aseema's work, came all the way from London to attend the function. Many of our students, alumni, and staff from Mumbai also attended it.

The Igatpuri students put up some wonderful performances—songs, dances, and a couple of skits. They performed confidently and enjoyed being on stage in front of the large audience.

Everyone who had been involved in the construction attended and a special mention was made of each of them and a token of appreciation was given to them. There were many speeches, the longest and most memorable one given by Biharilalji, who Punit had to eventually usher off the stage! It was a joyous and fulfilling occasion that ended with a delicious lunch.

The pre-primary school is lovely, small, and suitable for the young ones. There are three classrooms, a big multipurpose hall, and an office. There is also a room behind the office where I stayed whenever I visited Igatpuri and a couple of rooms in the basement to keep supplies and for additional activities. But the most charming feature was the central courtyard, where we conducted a little ceremony and planted the small champa (temple flower) tree gifted to us by our architect, Khushru. The tree is now very large and a constant reminder of our initial hope and prayer that it, together with our children, would grow, flower, and prosper.

The Central Courtyard

It was a pleasure working in the new building. The rooms were well-ventilated with a lot of light. The only problem was that all our funding had gone towards the construction of the building and there was no money left for furniture. Gradually, we were able to furnish room after room with second-hand, donated furniture. It took us a while to set up the classrooms, as each one had to be a perfect Montessori environment. Training of the teachers was now done by Nirmala Rao, as Chitra was not a Montessori teacher. She had done a wonderful job in the early years, but ultimately, we knew that we would follow the Montessori approach, as that is what we truly believe in. Jaya Glory, who had worked under Shalini Modi, spent a couple of months in Igatpuri introducing the teachers to the Montessori methods and principles until they were ready to carry on from there.

Attendance was still an issue and several incidents were responsible for this. Once, one of the adults in the village spread a rumour that we would convert all the children into Christians. For a couple of days, attendance dropped sharply. Another rumour that did the rounds said we would run away with all the children to Mumbai. Attendance was low again. Then came the oddest rumour of all—that the marriage of the girls who enrolled in our school would be delayed till the age of 40! In the tribal area where we work, girls are usually married at the age of 16 or 17 years, and sometimes even before that, so staying unmarried till 40 was a serious matter.

Each time Bhagubai would march to the people spreading these rumours and give them a piece of her mind. "Why are you doing this?" she would retort, "Do you not want your children to become clever and be educated?" Trying to make them feel ashamed of what they had done, she would add, "You and I have never been to school, so we don't know how to read or write. Do you want the same fate for the next generation?" Then she would explain to the parents, "Aseema has brought such a fine school to your doorstep. We must make the most of it. Please make sure your children attend from tomorrow or I will come to fetch them." Both she and Baban would continue to convince the parents until they started bringing their little children to school again.

The old classroom was now used as a dining room, and the small temporary kitchen became the school kitchen, where mid-day meals, that the children thoroughly enjoyed, were prepared.

As word about the school spread, it became a bit of a local attraction, with many people from Igatpuri simply coming to have a look at it. The plateau around the school was bare and had no plants and trees, so we started doing some gardening and plantation ourselves. Water was scarce, so we had to carefully select what we were planting.

We also employed people from the village to help clean and maintain the school daily and they were very happy to have employment. One such person was Sanjay Rere, who we noticed had worked very sincerely as a labourer with the construction team. He was mute and very intelligent, and he joined us as a gardener. Today, he is part of our larger garden team and its most artistic member. On occasion, we see Sanjay happily chatting with Mangesh Jadhav (from our Mumbai office) on his smartphone. Recently Mangesh, who is also mute, advised Sanjay to get a hearing aid, which helps Mangesh tremendously. It is amazing to see the two of them exchanging news—Mangesh in his usual friendly and animated style and Sanjay, much more subdued and shy. Watching them, I think of the time Mangesh joined us in 1999 when he was not even 18 years old. He lived opposite the Pali Chimbai Municipal School and when we got our first classroom and needed someone to clean and look after the class, one of the helpers in the school suggested Mangesh. He worked for about a year in the school and when we had our first office at G3 Josephine Apartments, he immediately came to me and indicated, "I want to work in the office, please." Initially, we had chosen another person for the task. But when he pleaded, I decided to give it a shot, not sure how well he would manage because of his disability. But soon we all realised that there was no need to worry; he was capable, hardworking, and could communicate better than most people!

Today Mangesh is married to Sukeshni, who is also mute. They have a young son, Yash, and a daughter, Anushka. I remember the time when Mangesh came very, very happily and proudly told me, "Yash is able to hear and talk." Anushka has a slight hearing impairment but is able to function perfectly well with a hearing aid.

Sanjay got married in the middle of the COVID-19 pandemic to a young tribal woman, Sunita and now has a young daughter. Looking at both Mangesh and Sanjay, I realise that their hearing disability is in fact no disability at all. They both seem happy and content and I sometimes wonder what their lives would have been like if they had not joined Aseema. But that is anyone's guess.

26

The Tribals of Awalkhed

"When the blood in your veins returns to the seas and the earth in your bones returns to the ground, perhaps then you will remember this land does not belong to you but you belong to the land."

– Native American Quote

Sanjay and many of our support staff are tribals who belong to the Thakur tribe. I always remember Advocate Pawar's words, "The Thakurs are very simple, honest people, and also very loyal," he told me at the time we purchased the land. "You will be very happy working with them." Until now, I have had no reason to doubt his words.

Schedule Tribes constitute 8.6 per cent of India's total population[4], and Maharashtra is home to 10.1 per cent of India's tribal population. While the all-India literacy rate is 73 per cent, the tribal literacy rate is 59 per cent. In Maharashtra, male literacy stands at 88.4 per cent, while tribal male literacy is 74.3 per cent. Female literacy in Maharashtra is 75.9 per cent, while tribal female literacy is only 57 per cent.[5]

In early 2016, Aseema conducted a survey of 230 households in Awalkhed village and the surrounding *wadis* to reassess the needs of the community. We found the following:

- 65% face extreme deprivation and insecurity
- 80% earn less than Rs. 5,000 (around 65 USD) per month
- 2.6% reach higher secondary level education

---

4   *Census 2011.*
5   *Report by the Ministry of Tribal Affairs, Government of India.*

- 79% drop out of school, the reasons being that they don't find school interesting; schools are not easily accessible; financial constraints; or the need to work at home.

The predominant occupation of the tribals is agriculture. Most of the farmers own little land and farming is possible only in the monsoon season from June to September, since no irrigation facilities are available. The produce is barely enough to satisfy the needs of the family for six months. The land lies parched and can be tilled for only four months each year. The tribals are without work and income for the remaining eight months.

Those who are not engaged in agriculture, work as contract labour or in construction. This can get them up to three days of work per week, but they need to be in constant touch with the contractor to know whether work is available.

Collecting and selling wood from the forest 12 kilometres away is another way of generating income, especially for women. They can earn up to Rs. 50 (65 US cents) per week. However, tribals, even those living in forest buffer zones, are routinely prevented from pursuing traditional forest occupations like collecting wood and constantly encounter opposition from forest officials.

Few families own about three to four animals—hens, goats, cows, or buffaloes. These are often sold to pay for medical bills or other emergencies. Hence, they are considered important assets. However, they commonly die of disease because of a lack of veterinary care.

There are no medical facilities in any of the *wadis* or villages. The closest health services are in Igatpuri—a municipal hospital or a private doctor. The municipal hospital lacks resources and thus, private clinics are preferred, even though they are expensive. *Bhagats* (or spiritual healers) are often their first port of call.

Large families have led to malnourishment of children, poor health of women, and scarcity of resources for the family. The houses, usually made of sticks and cow dung, have to be repaired annually, more often after the monsoons, which are among the heaviest in India. In recent years, every *wadi* has acquired an electricity connection, but many families cannot afford the bills and have cut their connection. Barring the exception of a couple of *wadis* (which were brought within the limits of the Igatpuri Municipal Council a few years ago), most of the *wadis* do not have any water connection. Common wells are at the foot of the hills, while the *wadis* are located at the top. Even these often dry up in summer.

The villages in this area lack basic amenities, such as clean drinking water and proper sanitation. Sadly, those who suffer most in this environment are the children. The harshness of their lives drives many community members to alcohol. Many children live with alcoholic fathers and witness domestic violence and abuse on a regular basis. Some of the children face pressure to start working at an early age. The situation for girls is even more challenging, with many restrictions and few opportunities.

Boy at the village well

An interesting project we undertook some years ago was "The Bicycle Project". We gave bicycles to many older children from the community, both girls and boys. Many of them walked a distance of almost nine kilometres each way, every day, to reach their schools or colleges in

Igatpuri town. The Zilla Parishad School (district council school) in Awalkhed only went up to Grade 6 at the time and the children had to complete their education at a school in Igatpuri town.

They trudged back and forth in the hot summer months and during the torrential monsoon and this resulted in many of them dropping out of school altogether. In an attempt to encourage them to continue with their studies, we decided to give them bicycles. But to make sure that they would value these, we took a nominal contribution from them. This would also enable us to make sure the bicycles were well maintained.

Nita Sanghvi, an ardent Aseema supporter and well-wisher, took the lead in this project and ensured that we were able to distribute 30 cycles to 30 deserving students. We often see these cycles being used not only by the students but also by other members of their families.

Adivasi Day

We started celebrating 'Adivasi Day' at our school in 2012. It is celebrated every year on the Tuesday closest to August 9, the United

Nations International Day of the World's Indigenous Peoples. (Farmers here have their weekly off on Tuesday.)

The cultural celebration at our school is attended by all the tribals in the vicinity. They attend in large numbers, sing their local songs and perform lively tribal dances. Our children also take part in this celebration and sing and dance with tremendous enthusiasm. Many of our staff, who are tribals, also perform with great gusto!

The women come in their traditional tribal clothes, bright red '*phadkis*' (traditional dress of the Thakur tribal women) with white dots and a floral green and yellow border, wrapped around them and covering their heads. This event has been taking place at our school for the past eight years and is looked forward to with much anticipation. It also gives the children and staff who are not tribals, a better understanding of tribal culture and customs. This is very important as it promotes respect for all religions and cultures.

A beautiful song that our children and the tribals often sing roughly translates to:

We the humble tribal people
Feel at ease with you.
Our beautiful school is in the valley and in nature
In that beautiful environment, teachers give us knowledge.
We the humble tribal people
Feel at ease with you.
Our parents are farmers and they are our breadwinners
Wages are in their homes.
We the humble tribal people
Feel at ease with you.
We have a mother in the form of nature
She brought the flame of knowledge to the village, for us.

27

An Amazing Water Diviner

"If you want others to be happy, practice compassion. If you want to be happy, practice compassion."

– Dalai Lama

Soon after the first 'Adivasi Day' was celebrated on August 9, 2012, Aseema got its first school bus. It was much needed to bring all the children to school and on time. Many of the children came from the surrounding *wadis*, but as word of the school spread, parents from other tribal communities and from Igatpuri town also sought admission. Preference was given to tribal children, but some economically disadvantaged children from the town were also admitted.

As the number of children increased, we started facing a shortage of water, despite having a well and the contour trenches and check dams we built years ago. The water table drops sharply during the hot summer and we were forced to start bringing in water tankers. It was at this time that we were introduced to Michael Davis, who was reputed to be an excellent water diviner. A well-wisher of Aseema, Kamal Moudawala suggested we take his advice and offered to cover his fees. "He is expensive," she told us, "but he is excellent."

Michael stayed at our school for four days and would spend the entire morning walking around the property with Prakash Kevhari, one of our gardeners, in tow. The afternoon was spent studying the plans of our property, and the evenings were spent talking. Michael loved to talk and had many interesting stories to share. He would tell us of the amazing work he had done in many parts of India and how he had time and again identified the exact spot to dig a borewell. "Sometimes water will spurt out like a fountain, and sometimes it will take time before it comes. One has to be patient," he would explain.

"In your case," he said, "a bore well will not work; we will have to go for an open well." Finally, on the fourth day, he identified the exact spot we were to dig the well. He took us down to the valley and showed us a place under a tree. "This is where you will have to blast," he said and made Prakash mark the exact spot with stones and a nail drilled into the ground.

"I use a simple method," he explained. He showed us a beautiful old-fashioned watch. "I use this watch; I study the path of the bees and the flow of water; I study the contour plan of the land, and most importantly, I pray. This is how I decide where the well should be located."

Michael was highly diabetic, so we had to take great care in the preparation of his meals. But there was one thing he could not resist, and that was a glass of beer every afternoon before lunch. So, we made sure he got his beer. After the marking was done, he left for Devlali, a small hill station in Maharashtra, where he lived part of the year.

Before leaving, he told us, "I have had a wonderful stay here and want you to know that I do not expect any fees from you. The work you are doing makes me very happy. Just one request—once you have made the well, please put a birdbath where the birds can come and have a drink." And he added, "Please start the work soon so that you have water at the earliest. Do keep me informed and let me know if you need any help." We started the work a few months later and followed all of Michael's instructions. It was difficult getting the work done in the valley, but we managed to make a road and got a JCB to go down. We also followed the specifications he had given. The biggest problem was that there was solid rock on one side of the well and soft *murrum* (earth) on the other side. As the workers continued with the blasting and went further down to remove the rocks, the soft *murrum* would fall on them making work very risky. We had to consult Michael once again.

"Increase the diameter to 30 feet. It will be easier for them to work," he explained, "and make a concrete ring inside."

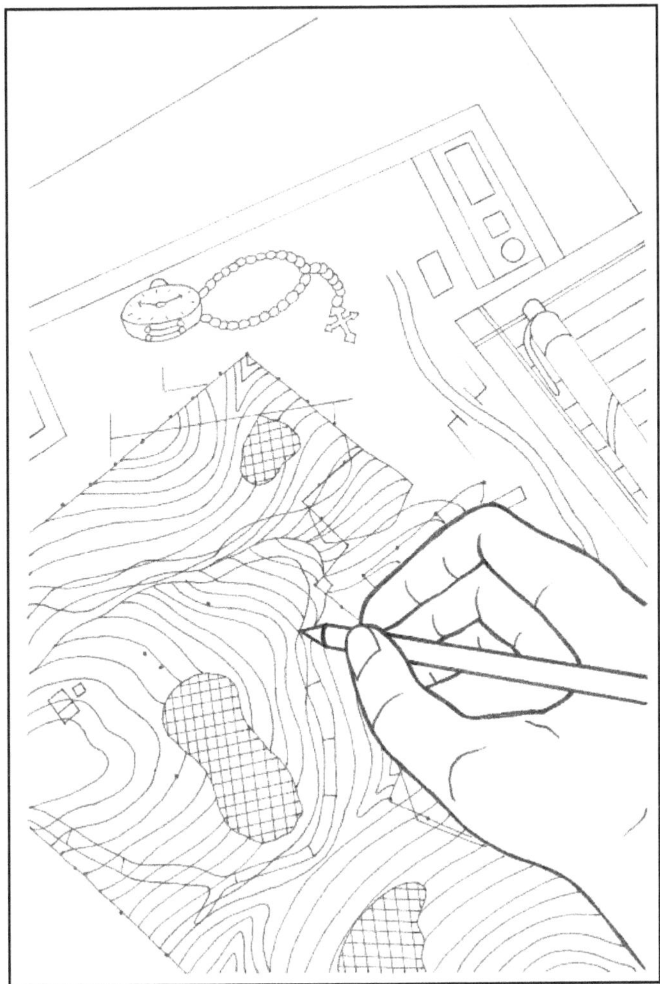

Michael studying the contour plan

He had wanted us to blast down to 50 feet, but this was not possible and the monsoon was fast approaching. Michael had been spot on and we soon struck considerable water in this well. A couple of years later, on the advice of a geologist, we continued digging further and went as far down as we could. It was sufficient and even today this is the well that provides the maximum water for the school.

The new well

Michael passed away a few years later. Whenever we see this well, we remember the happy time he spent with us at the school.

28

Pratham and NIOS

"Nothing in life is to be feared. It is only to be understood."

– Marie Curie

We started Aseema with one main objective—that children from marginalised communities should have access to relevant and meaningful education, which would build character and make them good human beings. The pedagogical approach we follow is based on the children's understanding, questioning, and thinking critically. This is very important for us and we were therefore initially reluctant to be affiliated with any one board of education. Being a Marathi-medium school, our options were further limited; we could either be affiliated with the Maharashtra State Board or the National Institute of Open Schooling (NIOS).

One of the members of our advisory board was Farida Lambay, a founder and trustee of the well-known non-governmental organisation, Pratham. Farida had been the Vice Principal of Nirmala Niketan College of Social Work and I had known her since then, as we employed many of their students as social workers at Aseema. Pratham ran NIOS centres across India. We consulted Farida, who agreed it was a good idea for our students to appear for the NIOS examinations. She also readily agreed to send her staff to our school to train our teachers.

The NIOS has Level A, which is equivalent to Grade 3; Level B is equivalent to Grade 5, and Level C is equivalent to Grade 8 of the State Board. After that, one could appear for the Grade 10 NIOS examination by registering online. On completion of that examination, students could go on to complete Grade 12 through NIOS or continue their studies at any college.

We found the NIOS curriculum to be quite interesting and meaningful and it also allowed us the freedom to engage in co-curricular activities like art and sports that are so important at Aseema. We were determined to avoid rote learning; the focus would not only be on the annual examination, but on the overall development of the child.

Sunita Veling and Pratibha Moparekar, two Pratham teachers, trained the Aseema teachers. Our children scored straight As in most of the Level A and B examinations. But there was a problem. No one in Igatpuri had ever heard of NIOS—not the local schools, nor the colleges, not even the officers of the education department. The Right to Education Act (RTE) came into force in 2010 and cast an obligation on the government and the local authorities to provide and ensure admission, attendance, and completion of elementary education to all children aged six to 14 years. It was a very important piece of legislation. With it, India moved forward to a rights-based framework that casts a legal obligation on the state to implement this fundamental right.

The lgatpuri education officers took the erroneous view that Aseema's Education Centre was illegal. This led to a stream of visits by the officers to our school, and correspondence for over three years asking us to close down the school, pay fines of Rs.1,000 per day and transfer the students to other 'legal' schools.

Rumours spread in the village that we were running a school without permission and that once the children finished their education, they would not get a valid school leaving certificate.

It was ironic—parents whose children were younger than four years old, parents who had never been to school themselves, and parents who continued to send their older daughters out with the cattle for grazing instead of to school, suddenly took a great interest in this 'leaving certificate', and a couple of them actually took their children away and admitted them to other schools.

One of our very committed and conscientious teachers, Yogita Pawar, was heartbroken when one of her students left. She had taken tremendous pains to coach a young girl who had great difficulty learning. All of a sudden, one day, the girl's father announced that he was not going to send her to our school ever again. When Pramila, one of our earliest students who had been with us since we had started the Anganwadi, saw how upset Yogita was she tried to console her, "Teacher, even if they all stop coming to school, I want you to know that I will continue to come." At that point, not only Yogita, but all of us shed a few tears.

Advocate Arvind Kothare (an expert on school matters), practising in the Bombay High Court, had been advising us throughout this ordeal and suggested that Aseema obtain an affiliation with the NIOS Board. We visited their regional office in Pune, got the requisite information, put together all the documents, and submitted the file. A visit was conducted by two of the NIOS officers a few months later. They were delighted with both the infrastructure and the quality of education and readily gave us permission to be a recognised NIOS centre. Meanwhile, certain events unfolded, which led us to get our school affiliated with the Maharashtra State Board. But more about that in a later chapter.

"What is man without the beasts?
If all the beasts were gone,
men would die from great loneliness of spirit
for whatever happens to the beasts also
happens to man. All things are connected.
Whatever befalls the earth befalls the
children of the earth."

29

Aseema Bal Shaikshanik Kendra (ABSK)

The students performed very well in the NIOS examinations and were involved in many other school activities. For the annual day celebrations, they would write scripts on topics of interest to them and perform them on stage. Since most of the children lived in Awalkhed village and the surrounding *wadis*, they were aware of the garbage dump being proposed in their village. They penned a script and performed it at the annual day celebration that year, expressing surprise at anyone who would consider setting up a garbage dump right next to a drinking water source. It was painful when they questioned, "What will be our fate if this really happens? Will we all have to leave our village if our water is polluted? Where will we go?"

They also took up topics like child labour, environmental issues like planting more trees and saving water, waste segregation, women's empowerment, the importance of education, and even loyalty to one's country and universal brotherhood. They were thinking and expressing themselves freely. The tribals are generally shy and not very expressive, so it was lovely to see them become more vocal, not with everyone, but at least with their teachers.

Danny Boyle with the students

Many visitors came to see the school and there was much excitement when Danny Boyle of *Slumdog Millionaire* fame visited. The children did not know much about him except that he had made a movie that had won many awards. But they enjoyed interacting with him! He was warm and friendly, and despite not knowing Marathi, was able to communicate quite well with them. The teachers were even more excited, and everyone wanted a photograph with 'Danny Sir'!

All the children, even the older ones affiliated with the NIOS, were accommodated in the pre-primary school building. What we had initially believed would be a very spacious building was now becoming increasingly crowded. I spoke to Neela, Snehal, and Nicola, who were trustees of Aseema at the time: "It's time for us to start considering our next phase of construction—the primary and secondary school building." In fact, we should have planned for it much earlier, but with all the challenges we had been facing with the garbage dump and the notices from the education office, we had decided to defer this initiative. Snehal offered sound advice: "We know how legal cases can drag on, we can't wait indefinitely. Best to start planning now."

Sanaa Shaikh and Natasha Albuquerque at the office started working on proposals and budgets and identifying potential donors, and Neela, the most artistic amongst us, suggested a few architects we could approach. We met a couple of them and finally decided on Ratan Batliboi, both for his experience and his approachable manner. He was a reputed architect and also the chairman of CRY, one of the first child rights non-governmental organisations in the country. We thought that such a person would be sensitive to our needs and understand what we were trying to do better than 'commercial' architects.

When we approached Ratan, we had no idea what the cost of putting up the whole school would be. At the time, we had not started approaching donors. "What will it cost us to build this school?" I ventured to ask at one of our earliest meetings. "How much have you got so far?" was Ratan's reply. On hearing our answer: "Nothing at the moment", he leaned far back in his chair and chuckled, "I love this. We will take up the project." And we knew we had come to the right person.

Soon after our first meeting, Ratan and his team visited the site. One of his first remarks was, "Your pre-primary building is very good. You have set a high standard and we will have to do even better than that." Reassuring words indeed!

The architects walked around the site and were delighted with the openness and energy of the place. Then followed a round of meetings in their office. We were made to think of every requirement, and this exercise went on for months. Mandar Karmarkar, one of Ratan's senior architects, and Supriya Chitale, his junior, worked on our project.

The Bhoomi Puja

After approving the initial design and plans, almost a year went by, selecting the contractor, the project management consultant, and the site engineer. Kaustubh Construction, led by Ashish Rathi, was appointed contractor. Deepak Bapodra and his assistant Nilesh Adurkar of R.S.V.A. Associates were the project management consultants and

Hemant Hire was appointed our site engineer. We had the *bhoomi puja* (a ceremony to mark the start of construction) on an auspicious day. A certain amount of site development was undertaken and construction finally started.

All new prospective donors wanted to visit the site, so my trips to Igatpuri became more frequent. The time I spent there was something I enjoyed very much. During the day, the teachers and staff had to be very careful with the children as construction had started. The children, too, understood the risks and observed all the rules, like not going to the side of the plateau where construction had begun, and walking in line when they went for breakfast and their midday meal.

We watched with great excitement as slab after slab was laid and the building slowly came up—the lower ground floor first, which housed the secondary classrooms, the science laboratory, the vocational, and resource rooms. Next, the ground floor where the admin office and staff rooms were located along with the lower primary classes, the library, and the medical and counselling rooms. Finally, the first floor had the upper primary classes and the computer laboratory. Right on top was a very large terrace with a magnificent view of the entire area. The plan was to eventually have art and music rooms on the terrace adjacent to an indoor sports area.

The building was at the far end of the plateau, diametrically opposite the entrance to the plot. Since it was on a slope, a lot of piling had to be done which, besides taking time, increased costs.

The steep slope before Awalkhed village made the transport of material cumbersome. Trucks found it difficult to climb and came only half-loaded. Occasionally, a fully loaded truck would be stuck on the slope and the construction workers would have to unload half the material before it could continue on its journey.

With the onset of the monsoon, construction slowed down. The lower ground floor was ready, and though much finishing work still remained to be done, we shifted some of the senior classes in this building, as the pre-primary school could not accommodate all the students any longer.

Along with construction and raising of funds for the new school, time was spent in the courts dealing with the troublesome garbage dump case. The notices from the education office also posed a problem, and it took up a lot of our time replying to each one.

We finally decided to meet the State Education Minister, Vinod Tawde, to appraise him of these matters. We showed him photographs of our school and he seemed pleased. "I know of Aseema's work," he said. "Since you are doing so much for the tribal children, I suggest you apply for state board recognition. It will help you greatly in the long run. Otherwise, you will keep facing problems from the education department."

Shambhavi Jogi, former Education Officer of the MCGM's Education Department, joined Aseema after her retirement in 2017. "It is a step in the right direction," she said. "A lot of paperwork will be required, but I know the procedure and what needs to be done." She prepared all the files and Renuka Lalwani from our office assisted by going to all the concerned government officers to follow up. In 2018, after almost a year and a half, we received affiliation to the state board.

The letters from the Igatpuri education department telling us we were illegal mercifully stopped! Parents too seemed satisfied, and Bhagubai declared, "This is wonderful! Madam, no one can now tell you to close down the school. This will be the best school in the whole of Nashik District!"

And we believe it is.

Etched into the hillside, the architecture of the building is a model of how to build in harmony with the natural landscape. With the lower ground floor at the base of the hill and the first floor at the plateau level, the building is an awe-inspiring sight. In addition, the basketball and football fields on campus have given the children access to state-of-the-art sports facilities.

In order to develop the campus and make it a model of sustainable growth, work has commenced in the areas of water harvesting, waste management, energy conservation, and plantation. Ajay Nayak and his team from Educated Environments (EdEn) advise us on these matters and work closely with our team in Igatpuri. We hope that this will encourage our students, their parents, and members of the tribal community to continue to live in harmony with nature.

30

The Tree of Life Grill and Furnishing the School

Once the construction was over, the beautiful grills created by Saravana D., a metal sculptor from Pondicherry, were installed. Now, with the finishing completed, it certainly looked like the most beautiful school in the district! A lot of work still remained though—we would need people who were committed to our cause, and a lot of teacher training, which would be a long and gradual process, but we were certainly on our way there!

The incredibly lovely 'Tree of Life' grill designed by Kirti Chandak, an artist in Pondicherry, and executed by Saravana took everyone's breath away. It is the first thing you see as you enter the school—the magnificent tree, around it the sun, flowers, leaves, birds, a butterfly, and even a snake! The entrance to the school is adorned on both sides by smaller grills with egrets, the white birds you see constantly in the sky above Awalkhed, or sitting on the buffaloes and cows pecking at the little insects on them.

Saravana, who lives in Pondicherry, came to Awalkhed to make these grills. "It will take me about two-and-a-half months," he initially told us. He stayed at the site and worked on the welding together with his assistant, a young tribal from the village. The metal with which they worked was spread all over the atrium while they worked. This went on and on and on. Two-and-a-half months turned to four, and the work was still not complete. The monsoon set in and Saravana, used to the sunny Pondicherry climate, was terribly homesick! "I will go home for a few days. I miss my mother and the Tamil food," he said, "but I will be back after a while." And so, he left with all the large pieces of metal spread over the entrance and atrium! A month passed and there was still no sign of Saravana.

Finally, after more than two months, when the monsoon had almost come to an end, Saravana returned and the entire construction team rejoiced! "Welcome back, Saravana! Tell us what is required and we will all help you," they said. Everyone was anxiously waiting for him to complete his work so that the rest of the finishing of the ground floor could be completed. But Saravana, the true artist that he was, worked at his own pace. The assistant left in frustration and we had to find another.

Then, finally, after another month and a half, the huge grill went up, and what a task it was putting it in place! It goes all the way from the ground floor to the second floor and needed 20 labourers to install. I call it a grill, but actually, it is almost a painting, a work of art. When Kirti came to Igatpuri and finally saw it in place, she said, "You have a real masterpiece here, no less." And everyone who enters the school for the first time simply stands and admires it for a while.

Once installed, Saravana was all set to leave. "But we have to paint it, and you, Saravana, have to guide the painters," I protested. It was no use. Punit assured me that we would get it done without Saravana. He had already packed his bags and Punit drove him to the station for the long train ride back to Pondicherry. "I will come back to put my signature on the grill," he said before leaving. He has not returned yet. But his beautiful grill continues to enthral us all, "Thank you, Saravana!"

Ramesh Ghayal, our alumnus, stepped in with two other friends to paint the grill. Kirti advised them on how it was to be done and supervised the finishing. Together with the two entrance egret grills, they were finally ready. Ramesh also made a lovely China mosaic 'champa' (temple flower) design on the resource block terrace.

We now have four buildings on the main plateau—the pre-primary school, the primary and secondary school, the resource person's block, and the kitchen and dining block. The most popular by far is the kitchen and dining block. While the kitchen is well-ventilated but completely closed, the dining room is a big cheerful room, open on three sides. The children not only enjoy going there for breakfast and lunch but also spend a little time after their meal interacting with their friends. It is a joy to watch them chatting and sunning themselves on the steps of the dining room on chilly winter days.

The new primary and secondary school is spacious and airy, with a lot of light. Fortunately, this time we had the funding to furnish the school. The school furniture from Infinity in Goa is well-designed and aesthetically pleasing. Once everything was in place, the children found it hard to believe it was all for them.

I remember when the first school bus came, a little boy inquired of his teacher, "Teacher, is this really for us? Are we going to ride on this bus?"

Women preparing the mid-day meal

Students in their new school bus

It was the same with the new desks and chairs. The children would sit on them very gingerly at first. The teachers, and especially the Assistant Head, Rushika Anare, were very particular and made sure the children looked after not only their desks and chairs but also their books and other belongings. Since the children were not used to having many of these facilities at home, they were reminded to use things carefully, for instance, not to waste water and electricity.

Here in school, water came out of a tap, which was new to them. They had seen their mothers trudging up and down the steep slope all their lives to fetch water daily. In many homes, there was no toilet, as open defecation was common. Here in school, many were seeing a toilet for the first time. Initially, the little ones would peer down the hole wondering what was in there. It took a while for them to understand and feel comfortable using it. When the government started a programme to build toilets in the homes of the tribals, many would use it as a cupboard to store their grains, so unfamiliar was the concept to them.

In the dining room, the children served themselves so that they learned to take only what they were able to eat. They were also encouraged not to waste anything.

It is a school which you will not see often in India, much less in a remote village. We could have built a school that was not quite as lovely. But there was a reason we did what we did. Overall, the materials used were simple Kota stone and regular tiles. But we did want to have beauty in the school and it took a lot of time and energy to ensure the details were taken care of.

Having a lovely, welcoming place to come to every day gives students a sense of security and a desire to remain there. It can boost their self-esteem, resulting in increased focus, involvement, and enjoyment. For many children, entering a classroom that has been purposefully constructed delivers the message that they matter, that they are valued, and that they can be encouraged and empowered to take charge of their own learning.

Over the years, I have observed that many people believe that just anything will do for the poor. "Why are you giving them such good art paper and paints?" they often ask. "Just take this; it is not such good quality but it will do for them."

"Why will it do for them and not for you or your children?" I'd think.

When we built the first toilets at the Pali Chimbai Municipal School, some people had disparagingly called them "5-Star toilets", implying that clean and well-designed toilets were not needed for children in these schools. The toilets were nothing fancy, just simple tiles, but of good quality and yes, our children had worked with the students of a graphic art course at Sophia College and created lovely art on some of the tiles. These painted and fired tiles had been put up in an interesting way by Varsha, the art teacher, which made the area look very beautiful.

The worst that I have ever heard on the subject was when a headmistress of one such school told me, "Why do you all pay so much attention to these children? They have come from the gutters, and will always remain there." That was in the very early years, but it is a remark that I have never forgotten. I was too shocked and upset to even reply.

I have been fortunate to have been able to create a team—my core team, teachers, support staff, volunteers, and well-wishers who believe that the children deserve the best. We have also been fortunate to have trustees, advisors, and above all, donors who trust us and have faith in our beliefs and way of thinking and working.

If they are as disadvantaged as our children are, and if they have to collaborate (not compete) with other children, do they not need facilities that are as good as the children from privileged families? Over the years, we have always said that our children have only to be given the right opportunities and they will do as well as children anywhere, if not better. Will this not equip them greatly when they go out into the world? Do we not want to create a more egalitarian world, a better world?

31

The Inauguration of ABSK

"Whatever you do, try to do it like nobody else has done it before."

Finally, it was time for the inauguration of the new building. We decided to have it on Aseema's birthday, December 15, the day we had started our education centre at St. Stanislaus High School. Again, there were many people to be invited, so we decided to have the function for over two days. Punit was in charge at the Igatpuri end and Sabina Talpade, our office administrator, at the Mumbai end. For an event of this scale, we were advised to appoint a professional agency, but we preferred to handle it ourselves. This was firstly, to give it a personal touch and secondly, because such agencies can be very expensive, and as usual, we were trying to manage with a very limited budget.

The chief guest on this occasion was the Minister for School Education, Vinod Tawde, who had been a great support. Following the custom in Igatpuri, we invited several guests of honour and special guests.

Almost 1,000 people were expected to attend over the two days, so there was much to be done. Many of the office staff and key school staff from Mumbai went a couple of days in advance to assist the staff in Igatpuri.

A beautiful shamiana-like structure was erected in front of the stage to protect the guests from the sun. Though it was winter, and cold at night, the sun on the exposed plateau could be scorching during the day.

Arrangements were made for flower decorations and beautiful 'rangolis', (designs made on the ground with colourful powder) as is the custom in India on all auspicious occasions. The children were made to rehearse their songs, dances and plays till they were perfect. Everyone was busy, happy and excited, but also anxious. It was a very important occasion for us.

Just one day before the inauguration, there were cyclonic conditions in Igatpuri and the wind swept everything away. We hoped and prayed that the storm would blow over, but nothing of the sort. We woke up very early on December 15 to witness the shamiana ripped to shreds. The poles stood erect, but the remnants of the once beautiful frills and decorations of the shamiana had to be removed from the poles. It was so windy that morning that the carpets and the chairs for the guests too could not be arranged; everything was flying all over the place. The beautiful marigold garlands we had made refused to stay in place, and the 'rangolis' were just blown off.

The Education Minister was expected at 10:30 a.m. At 10:10 a.m., we received a call that he was already in the village of Awalkhed and would arrive any minute. It was chaotic at the site and I still remember saying in a panic to Sabina, "What on earth are we going to do?" She too seemed unnerved, but bravely told me, "Don't worry, everything will be fine. You please go and attend to the guests." Then she quickly added, "But let's pray." Neela, my dear friend and co-trustee, simply said, "There is nothing we can do. Just be calm and everything will be okay." I was a complete bundle of nerves.

The minister arrived at 10.20 a.m., ahead of schedule, together with a special guest, Shyam Jaju, a politician, who had especially come from New Delhi for the function. Neela and I took them and another special guest, Rajaram Mane, the Divisional Commissioner, Nashik, into the school for breakfast. The breakfast was delicious but neither Neela nor I could enjoy it, our minds were on the chaos outside! Our master of ceremonies, Shyama Kulkarni, an ardent Aseema supporter, who had known the minister for many years, joined us and with breakfast finally over, we nervously ventured out, unsure of what was in store for us.

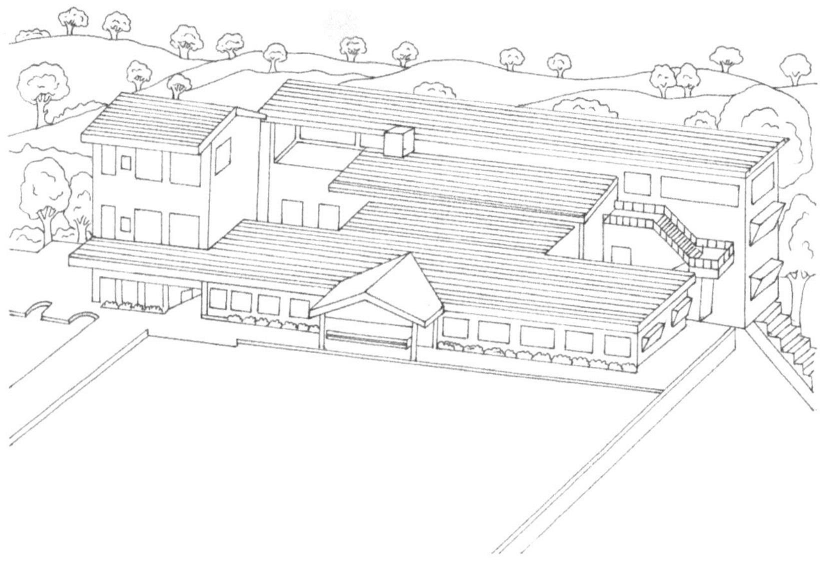

The Primary and Secondary School Building

It was a windy walk from the pre-primary, where we had breakfast, to the new school building where the inaugural lamp was to be lit and the red ribbon untied. The minister stopped on the way to interact with the children who were sitting on the basketball court alongside the stage.

"What do you do in school?" he asked, to which they replied, "Oh, we sing and dance and play." There was no mention of studies!

Finally, the beautiful music from 'Divine Gypsy' was played—our cue to lead the minister inside the new building. There was a huge crowd at the entrance by then. Many people had gatecrashed the school in their enthusiasm to meet the minister and there was nothing we could do to stop them. The lamp was lit, the red ribbon untied, the '*khond shil*' (inaugural plaque) unveiled, and the minister and all the special invitees were taken around the new school building. "It is well done," he remarked as soon as he entered. "You will have to look after and maintain this place very well. It's a wonderful opportunity for the children and they must make the most of it."

After a short tour of the building, he said, "Let us go and start the programme. I have an important meeting in Mumbai and have to leave in an hour."

When we stepped out of the building and headed to the stage, it was as if a miracle had happened. Everything was in place and in order. All but the beautiful shamiana. Only the poles remained, but no one seemed to notice or mind. Everyone was in high spirits and the wind had also settled down. The sun was not at full height, so it was cool and pleasant and later, even when it shone brightly, the mood was uplifting.

The function started with a dance performance by our girls from Mumbai, followed by songs, dances and plays performed by the Igatpuri children. Everything went like clockwork and the children were wonderful! Three of our alumni from the Mumbai schools spoke about how education had changed their lives and so did two of our older students from Igatpuri. Shy at first, they soon gained confidence and spoke straight from the heart.

The chief guest's speech emphasised the value of education. Many of the special guests, including our donors, spoke too. Finally, it was time for the vote of thanks, with Aseema gifts being given to all who had contributed to the event. The joyous occasion ended with a delicious lunch prepared by the Igatpuri caterer Mangilal, who went out of his way to please us, under Sabina's strict supervision and watchful eye.

After all the guests had left, we heaved a sigh of relief that everything had gone so well. The day, which had started somewhat inauspiciously, had a splendid ending. But not quite. That evening, a basketball match was organised between the children and some of the adults. Overjoyed at the events of the day, in my enthusiasm, while running after the ball, I had a bad fall and fell flat on my face! I initially thought I had broken all my teeth and dislocated my jaw. There was a deep cut just below my chin, which was bleeding profusely, and I was rushed to the doctor in Igatpuri town.

After cleaning and bandaging the wound, I was given a tetanus shot. Neela, Punit, and Geeta accompanied me to the doctor and I will always remember the manner in which Geeta comforted me after the fall and on the drive to the doctor and back. I was in a state of shock, and her words and manner were extremely comforting and reassuring. I remember thinking to myself, "Geeta is really the right person to head the big and difficult Kherwadi Municipal School. She must be giving the children the same loving care when they are injured." The doctor had advised complete rest, so on getting back to school, I went directly to my room.

Fortunately, my sister Arnavaz and my niece Zia were there to take good care of me. Many of my colleagues from Mumbai, who were also staying at school and all the Igatpuri staff, were upset at what had happened. I felt dreadful that I was the cause of so much distress. At the same time, I was worried, as my whole face and jaw felt very strange. But there was also a feeling of great relief and satisfaction that everything had gone so well that day.

Bhagubai was probably the most upset of all. "How are you feeling, madam?" she inquired. For once she spoke softly, seeing me lying quietly in bed. "Please rest," she added. She firmly believed that an evil eye had been cast over me and proceeded to take a lemon and circle it a couple of times over me, and then throw it out of the window near the trees below. "There was no need for you to play basketball, madam," she chided. Bhagubai was being polite—what she probably meant was that at my age, one does not play basketball! She was so right. I have never been the sporting kind, but everyone had been having so much fun that I too decided to join in with great gusto!

The next day was another function for the entire village, the students, teachers, alumni and well-wishers from Mumbai. The Tehsildar was the chief guest, and the Guests of Honour were the Sarpanch, Mangabai Shid, the Deputy Sarpanch, our very own Bhagubai Pawar, the Police Patil, Deepali Pawar and the Gram Sevika, Rupali Jadhav. The children repeated the performances and then we had speeches by the Chief Guest and Guests of Honour.

We returned to Mumbai that evening. Fortunately, my wounds healed fast, but the dental treatment took months. It was a great relief when the dental surgeon saw the X-ray and said, "Normally in this kind of fall, one fractures the jaw. You have been very lucky." I realised that God had been very kind indeed.

On the evening of the inauguration, a teacher from Igatpuri remarked: "Toil, sweat, tears, and blood have gone into the making of this school. And today we have seen the last, the blood." I hoped and prayed, "Toil and sweat we are prepared to continue with, but oh Lord, may this be the last of the tears and blood!"

SECTION V

GENERAL

32

Health and Nutrition

We continue to create an environment that emphasises holistic growth, values compassion and celebrates the little victories of each day.

In the course of our work with the children, we were determined not to lose focus. Education was our core purpose and there was so much to be done in that field that we could not divert our time and energy to other areas. This is what we strived for and believed. But so many other issues started emerging: Children falling ill, lack of proper nutrition and family problems that adversely impacted the child's emotional health. We realised that we simply could not ignore these, as they all had a direct impact on the child's learning.

How could a child who is hungry focus on his studies?

How could a sick child concentrate on her work?

How could a child who had faced or even witnessed abuse at home learn?

Nutrition

This led us to start with simple things like giving the children bananas whenever we could afford them. The doctor who visited our centre at St. Stanislaus in the early years had advised: "It is far better for you to spend whatever money you have on nutrition rather than medicines." Well-wishers contributed and eventually, we were able to offer dinner to the children every evening, something they really looked forward to.

Children serving themselves in the dining room

We still fondly remember the kind 'Russel Sir', who provided our children with dinner at St. Stanislaus High School. It used to be a real treat, with even chicken being provided on special occasions, which the children so loved. In the early years, we had also noticed that when the children came back to school after their summer and Diwali vacations—these being the two long holidays—they always looked thinner.

Today, many years later, we continue to give the children a nutritious meal daily. We have prepared a balanced menu that is strictly followed. The children in Igatpuri get both breakfast and lunch. We have seen that the nutrition programme has helped the children overcome malnourishment. The meal is wholesome and tasty and very much looked forward to. Sometimes we find little notes left by the children in the children's feedback box that say, "Please don't give us *khichdi* (a dish of rice and lentils) so often, can you instead give us *biryani* (a spicy rice dish made with fish, eggs, chicken or vegetables) once a month?"

We try to accommodate all reasonable food requests from the children, provided they fit within our budget and are healthy. A banana is also given daily to every child in Mumbai, and occasionally oranges and guava, when in season. In Igatpuri, papaya or melon is served at breakfast time, and the children enjoy these fruits very much.

Physical Education

Physical education is given great importance at Aseema. All our children participate in an hour of sports every day. Many of them have excelled in sports and won many medals at inter-school and state-level competitions in judo, handball, rugby, athletics, volleyball, kho-kho, wrestling, and carrom. Two students participated at the national level in rugby and judo. While winning medals is good, even more important for us is what this does for the child's physical development, well-being, and spirit of sportsmanship.

A physical education class

Health

Health is another area that needs great attention. Many of our children live in unhygienic environments. Their parents struggle to make ends meet. Spending on quality education or medical treatment is a luxury many cannot even imagine. When there is a medical problem, they visit government hospitals that have very good doctors but are usually overcrowded and poorly maintained. Children often have skin infections, and they suffer from common colds, fever, etc. Sometimes the issue is serious. We have had children who succumbed to dengue simply because they did not receive proper treatment on time.

In Igatpuri, the situation is even more trying, as many parents prefer to visit the local *'bhagat'* (spiritual healer) when sick, rather than go to a doctor. We had the case of a seven-year-old girl who fell while playing outside her home and fractured her arm. No amount of coaxing could convince the parents to take her to a doctor. They took her to the local *'bhagat'* instead, who gave them some herbs and ointment to apply on her fractured arm.

Since she was unable to come to school, our social worker and teachers visited the little girl at home. There was absolutely no improvement in her condition, and she continued to suffer in great pain. But the parents remained unmoved, as they firmly believed the herbs and balm would heal the fractured bone. Three weeks later, when there was still no improvement, I went to see her. The swelling was prominent and the arm now looked crooked. This time, the parents agreed to let us take her to the doctor, who explained how the bone had been set incorrectly. It was quite a procedure to rectify the problem, which caused the child even more pain and trauma. Finally, after a couple of months, the troublesome arm healed.

While we know the efficacy of local plants and herbs in treating some ailments, other health challenges need medical intervention. It is for this reason that we organise medical camps at the school every three months. A team of doctors from Nashik—a general physician, a paediatrician, a gynaecologist, and on occasion an ophthalmologist and dentist, examine the children and prescribe treatment when required. Thanks to these camps, we have been able to identify children who have serious problems like diabetes, convulsions, trophic ulcers, rheumatism, and even heart ailments. For serious medical issues, the child has to be taken to Nashik or Mumbai as the medical facilities in Igatpuri are inadequate

During medical camps, even the parents are invited and the doctors give a talk on a subject relevant to them to make parents aware of the importance of getting medical attention in time. Simple home remedies are also shared for cases which are not serious and the importance of good nutrition and hygiene is emphasised.

During Diwali and other festivals, some of our donors like to give the children something special, like a sweet or special food item, which is much appreciated. Today, a lot of people prefer to donate money for a special meal for our children on their birthdays or anniversaries, rather than having a big party themselves.

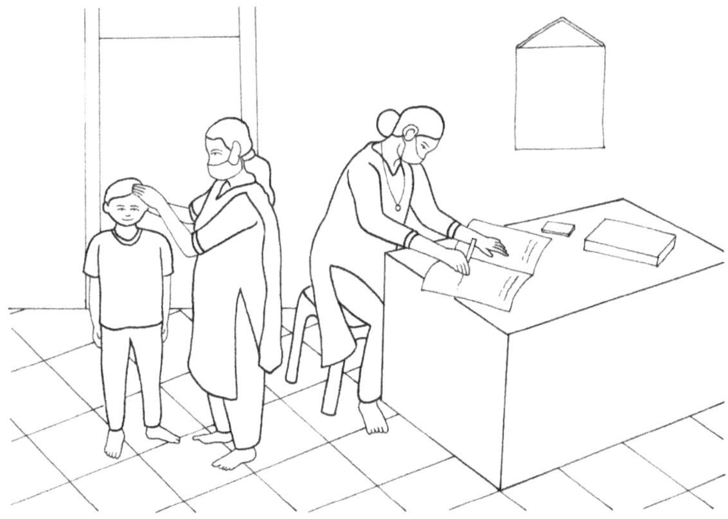

A medical camp in progress

One corporate donor sends boxes of dry fruits and nuts for the children every Diwali. An Aseema alumnus, had this to share: "Aseema provides not only education but also food to the students. Most of the students at Aseema are below the poverty line and don't have food at home. The ones who do not eat at home can at least have lunch in school, which is still enough for survival." Then he went on to add, "The last time I visited my school they were giving dry fruits to the students. I liked that very much!"

Emotional Health

This plays a very important part in our work at Aseema. It is also one of the most difficult issues to handle. We started many years ago by having a child psychotherapist, Zarine D'Monte, taking weekly sessions with us. At the time, we were just a few people—teachers and some of us at the office. We would talk about cases of abuse, neglect, disturbed or withdrawn behaviour and violence that we encountered and Ms D'Monte would probe further, making us seek the answers ourselves. This went on for several years. She was trained at the reputed Tavistock School of Psychotherapy and we found the discussions we had with her both interesting and of great value. We learned there were no immediate answers or solutions. It was a slow process, sometimes painfully slow. But as she often told us, "You have to get to the root of the problem, not simply skim the surface."

The discussions we had with Ms D'Monte over the years encouraged us to launch a counselling centre at Aseema. At first, we could afford only one counsellor. Then, thanks to support from a corporate donor, who also understood the importance of emotional well-being, we appointed counsellors in all our schools. Counsellors too were not easy to find, particularly the kind that Ms. D'Monte approved of, those who would "not simply skim the surface."

"Given their home environment," she would tell us, "it is a wonder that the children are learning at all." She would often point out, "You need to look at education differently." These words have stayed with me and led us to further explore what quality education means. What is the goal and purpose of education? This became the foundation for our education approach.

We have had many difficult cases over the years, mainly of children being very disruptive in class and even violent. There have been other cases of children being very quiet and withdrawn, and a few cases of manipulative children. A few times, we have also had to refer the case to a psychiatrist while continuing with the counselling sessions. Parents, too, are called for sessions separately. By and large, we have found that they cooperate. Those who refuse to cooperate or are in denial make the case even more complicated and solutions are then difficult to find.

The stigma attached to mental and emotional health even today makes it a challenge to handle such cases. But we have come a long way and now, even though most of the cases are still referred to by the teachers, some of the children come on their own to talk to the counsellor.

We continue to strive to create an environment that emphasises holistic growth, values compassion and celebrates the little victories of each day.

33

Aseema's Education Approach

*"Give the pupils something to do, not something to learn;
and the doing is of such a nature as to demand thinking;
learning naturally results."*

– John Dewey

The 'How-to-live' Philosophy of Paramahansa Yogananda

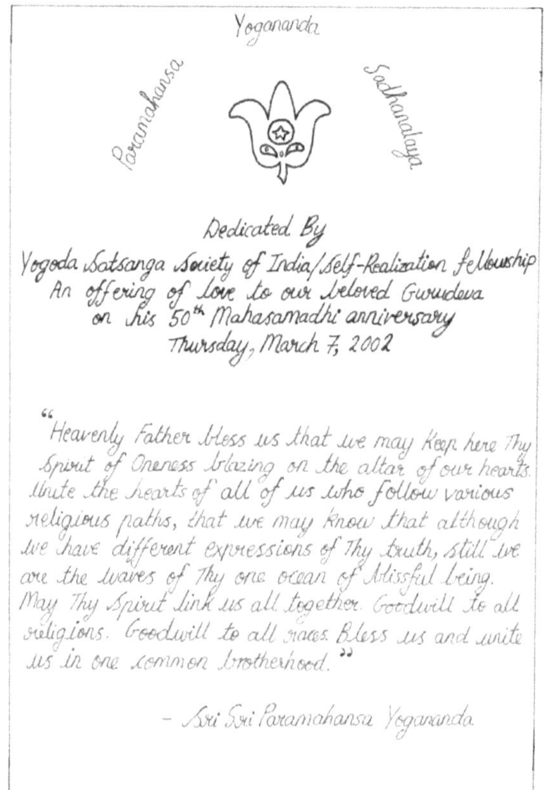

Our approach to education has evolved. In the very early years, the
focus was on developing values like honesty, patience, simplicity,

compassion, humility, love, gratitude and so on, based on the 'How-to-live' philosophy of Paramahansa Yogananda. We integrated these values into everything we did. The adults tried to be role models to the children and lived by these principles in the hope that the children would imbibe these values and make them a part of their lives. Over the years, we have seen that when the teacher herself is responsible and disciplined, the child simply follows her example and discovers what it means to live in true freedom.

The Atmananda Memorial School

Bond between the teacher and the child

After visiting the Atmananda Memorial School in Kerala, we realised the great importance of the 'bond between the teacher and the child' in learning. We understood that the child's emotional needs were paramount; learning simply could not happen unless the child felt safe and secure. The knowledge that she is valued and that her thoughts matter is the most empowering gift that you can give a child.

The Montessori Approach

The Montessori approach, which we follow very closely at Aseema, particularly in the pre-primary section, only strengthened our faith and belief that what we had been doing since inception was the kind of education we sorely needed. Value education had to be coupled with achieving high standards in academics. The Montessori approach spoke about that blend.

It showed us how schools could help children become active learners, prepare them for the world of change in which we live and give them the skills required for solving problems in the real world.

Montessori education contains three essential elements: A prepared environment, a prepared adult, and freedom with responsibility.

The prepared environment is always a place of simplicity, beauty, and order. The thoughtful arrangement of the classroom is very important—it needs to be uncluttered and conducive to activity and concentration. The Montessori apparatus helps the child's development through a process of exploration and discovery. The children at Aseema have always responded to the material with enthusiasm and delight and take great care in looking after it.

Observation of the child is critical, and it is in the children's independent use of the materials (after the teacher has presented it) that learning takes place.

A comment that we sometimes hear from the Aseema teachers who are new or who haven't fully understood our approach is, "Oh, the children are free to do whatever they want. We can't say no to them, and that is why some of them are so indisciplined." This is a complete misunderstanding of the approach.

Freedom does not mean allowing the child to do whatever he or she wants. If we were to allow their every whim and fancy, it could be harmful not only to them but also to the other children and the environment. The teacher has to ensure that the child is engaged in meaningful activity and not just squandering her time or disturbing the other children.

Maria Montessori defined the goal of education as: "The development of a complete human being, oriented to the environment and adapted to his or her time, place, and culture."

Today, there are over 15,000 Montessori schools all over the world and their number continues to increase. In India, there are 159 Montessori schools. These schools cater mostly to children from well-to-do families. To the best of my knowledge, Aseema is the first and only organisation in India to follow the Montessori approach in schools for children from marginalised communities.

Children working with the Montessori apparatus

The pre-primary class has a mixed age group of children—two-and-a-half to six years—as so much indirect learning occurs both for the very little ones and the older children. There is also only one set of material the children are expected to share between them. This helps them learn patience and respect for others as they wait for the material to be back on the shelf.

Dr Montessori explained the method in this way: "All these little things help. They bring sympathy and understanding. It gradually brings a real harmony which could not be given artificially."

Also, since the children remain with one teacher for three years before going to the higher class, "It brings about a depth of relationship, positive influence by the teacher and modelling of behaviour are greatly increased." In these three years, the teacher has to be patient, persevere and have faith that each child will develop at her or his own pace.

Maria Montessori firmly believed that children as young as three years show a desire for concentrated work. Once this desire is fulfilled, they become calmer and content. "It is by work that children organise their personalities," she used to say.

The focus in the pre-primary years is on the sensitive periods in which the child appears to be working on one specific area of development, to the exclusion of all others. The focus is also on the absorbent mind. The child soaks in like a sponge whatever there is—good or bad, beautiful or ugly, peaceful or violent.

Of primary importance is the child's development of good manners, gentleness with each other, confidence and ease with those both younger and older than themselves, including adults, their care of the environment, and their eagerness and energy for learning.

We have tried to incorporate many of Montessori's ideas and principles in our pre-primary centres in Mumbai and Igatpuri. In Mumbai, we have been able to employ trained Montessori teachers, while in Igatpuri we have had to train them ourselves.

Having witnessed the success of the Montessori approach in the pre-primary environment, we were convinced that it needed to be taken further into the primary section.

Activity-Based Learning in the Primary Section

We were fortunate to have Andrea Nunes join us at the time we decided to incorporate Montessori principles in the primary section. Andrea had been a teacher in our pre-primary class for a couple of years before she went on to do the elementary Montessori course, which is for six to 12-year-olds. She shared what she learned with our teachers over two years and we did our best to incorporate the learnings in Grades 1 to 7 of our Mumbai schools. It was quite a challenge as MCGM officials are averse to anything but the state board books being closely followed.

Around the same time, we set up a training team at Aseema and started work on manuals that would help the teachers teach effectively and collaboratively.

Most of our teachers are B.Ed. teachers from different educational institutes in Mumbai. They are accustomed to teaching from state board textbooks. These books are not very well designed and they do not promote thinking, questioning or analysing skills. Our training team, under Andrea's guidance, took concepts that needed to be learnt and introduced as many Montessori principles and activities as possible to teach these concepts.

At the elementary level (equivalent to Grades 1 to 7), the absorbent mind and sensitive periods of the earlier years are replaced with new abilities. The children now have immense mental stamina and are capable of great effort and concentration. They want to grasp what knowledge they can and enjoy overcoming obstacles and facing challenges. Maria Montessori called this phase 'the Intellectual Period'.

Children begin to distance themselves from their families, form their own peer groups and become more extroverted. Their good manners of earlier years also become unpredictable. Their interest is now in distinguishing right from wrong. "It is at this age that the concept of justice is born," said Maria Montessori. This interest in morality and justice leads to a tendency to worship heroes. There is intense interest and admiration for great men and women who have pushed to the limits of human capabilities.

A yoga class in progress

One of their greatest new powers is their capacity for imagination. Maria Montessori emphasised that at this stage: "Our aim, therefore, is not merely to make the child understand, and still less to force them to memorise, but to so touch their imagination as to enthuse them to their innermost core. We do not want complacent pupils, but eager ones; we seek to sow life in children rather than theories, to help them in their growth—mental and emotional as well as physical."

Hence, Montessori designed five major stories (The Great Lessons), and numerous minor ones to introduce the universe to children. These stories give just enough to create the beginning of an interest. The goal of the lessons is to lead the child to lifelong learning.

1. The first Great Lesson is, 'The Creation of the Universe and Coming into Being of Earth'.
2. The second Great Lesson is called 'The Coming of Life'. It tells the story of life on Earth and introduces children to the study of biology.

3. The third Great Lesson is called 'The Coming of Human Beings' and it introduces them to the study of history and the progress of human civilisation.

4. The fourth Great Lesson is 'The Story of Communication in Signs', and

5. The fifth is 'The Story of Numbers'.

All the Great Lessons are given within six to eight weeks of starting school. As the purpose of the Great Lessons is to arouse the children's imagination, they are not followed with assignments, but by what Montessori calls 'the rest'. The children are left alone for a period of calm and reflection to think about what they have heard and seen.

While we have attempted to do some of the above in primary classes at Aseema, much remains to be done. In future years, we also hope to be able to study Montessori's thoughts for adolescents and young adults to see if we could incorporate some of what she had researched and taught into our work with the children.

Integral Education as Envisaged by Sri Aurobindo and The Mother of Pondicherry

Another education philosophy that we apply to our work is integral education. The Sri Aurobindo International Centre for Education (SAICE) is an inspirational school in Pondicherry, and many of our teachers undergo the Teacher's Training Course conducted every year by the Sri Aurobindo Society.

In integral education, the first principle of true teaching is that nothing can be taught. The teacher is not an instructor and does not impart knowledge to the pupil. He or she only helps and guides the child and shows her how to acquire knowledge.

An integral teacher is a guide and a guru to oneself and to all others. It demands an absolute and lifelong commitment to learning and growing. At the heart of integral education is the belief that learning happens more through nurturing relationships than as a result of a definite pedagogy. Thus, creating relationships that enable learning is of the greatest importance. Every child has within her the fullest potential for her highest evolution. All that she needs to learn is already within her and only needs to be drawn out. The teacher has to simply awaken in children an urge to learn and create an environment that encourages exploration and enquiry.

The second basic principle of integral education is that the mind has to be consulted for its own growth. A culture where the learner is a conscious, volitional being who has an innate sense of what she needs and wants to learn needs to be created. She has to be personally involved in the learning process. An effective way to create a sustainable participative culture is through dialogue and discussion. The importance of these in classroom teaching cannot be emphasised enough. The aim is to lead the child to solutions, to facilitate the learning process and to not kill the child's interest. The teacher has to be sensitive enough to know when to lead a child on and when to let the child struggle and discover for herself.

The third fundamental principle of integral education is the idea of working from 'the near' to 'the far'. The principle of relevance is an important one in integral education. Most children fail to assimilate their learning when they do not feel connected to what they are being taught. We learn best what we need most to learn. Even when the learning need is academic, it should be related to a real-life necessity.

An Amalgamation of These Approaches

Aseema's education approach has evolved over the years and contains elements of the philosophies mentioned above. One simple book we have referred to over the years and encouraged all our staff to read is *Totto-Chan* by Tetsuko Kuroyanagi. It is the story of a little girl, Totto-Chan, who attends a unique school in Tokyo, Japan during World War II. This unconventional school, Tomoe Gakuen, combined learning with fun, freedom, and love and was run by an extraordinary educationist, Sosaku Kobayashi, its founder and headmaster. The book and the approach followed by this visionary man continue to inspire us in all that we do at Aseema.

The teachings of Paramahansa Yogananda, Dr Maria Montessori, Sri Aurobindo, The Mother, and the Atmananda Memorial School all have a spiritual base, and their goal is to create responsible human beings who care for themselves, their families, their community, their environment and the world at large.

34

Vision and Mission

Realise Human Potential Through Quality Education.

When Aseema was established in 1995, we drafted a trust deed that listed our objectives, the responsibilities of trustees and other details. Subsequently, we amended it to elaborate on some of our core objectives and goals.

In the early years, donors asked for proposals and reports, but not for too many other details. As we grew larger and attracted more people to work with us, we realised everyone did not have the same understanding, commitment and passion towards their work. Donors too asked about our vision, our mission and our goals and we knew it was time to articulate these. It would give people clarity and provide a framework within which to work.

Sanaa Shaikh was our chief operating officer (COO) at the time, and she took on this important task. We consulted the NGO, United Way of Mumbai, and they guided us through this process.

It started with the trustees having to articulate their vision for the organisation, which we did. The next step was conversations with the entire staff, about 150 at the time—teachers, office, and support staff. Meetings of about 10–12 people in each batch were held, and they were asked about their thoughts and goals for themselves and the organisation.

All this finally culminated in our vision and mission statements:

Our Vision: To realise human potential through quality education.

Our Mission: To equip children from marginalised communities with high-quality, value-based education enabling the development of their limitless potential.

Our pillars and goals are:

1. **Pillar**: Building a nurturing environment

   Goals: a. Providing the ideal physical environment for learning

   b. Ensuring the emotional well-being of every child

2. **Pillar**: Adopting excellent teaching-learning methodologies

   Goals: a. Implementing a high-quality teaching approach

   b. Offering a well-rounded curriculum

3. **Pillar**: Fostering community partnerships

   Goals: a. Increasing family and neighbourhood participation

   b. Increasing impact through sharing of learning

Actions that need to be taken to achieve these goals are also clearly defined.

In mid-2014, the vision, mission, goals, and actions were shared with the entire Aseema family. This provided the framework for all that we were doing and would do in the future and also provided concise and transparent information about Aseema to its donors.

The document is so well drafted that in 2019 when we had a review of all that we were doing, we adopted the same goals and actions. We also realised that we still had much work to do to ensure the effective implementation of each goal and action. But what is important is that this document gives clarity and provides a clear understanding of what Aseema stands for and believes in. And for this, many thanks to dear Sanaa!

35

Early Students

"There is no higher calling in terms of a career than public service, which is a chance to make a difference in people's lives and improve the world."

Mamta Aeidurappa's story in her own words:

I grew up living in a slum at Bandra Reclamation. The place was filled with alcoholics and bad people who used to drink and gamble all day, and this is what I grew up seeing.

My father was also an alcoholic, and he used to beat us children and our mummy a lot. We are six children and life was very difficult. For our parents, giving us food was much more important than giving us education.

My parents sent us to school so that we remained safe when they went to work. When I was very young, I attended a municipal school where the teachers just came into the class and walked out without teaching anything.

A day came when Dilbur teacher came into this slum and convinced our parents to send the children to learn with her. My journey began in Aseema when I was nine years old.

We started going to St. Stanislaus School, where one room was given to us to study. I remember there were some times when we were not allowed to use the classroom there. So, a small group of children were picked up by Shobha didi and we were taken to a garden where stories and basic things used to be taught to us by Dilbur, Tasneem, and Alice teacher. We usually were given a banana after class.

All the children used to go home with something that they learned that day. Parents started having faith in the fact that there was something interesting happening with their children.

At that time, Aseema did not have a formal school. So, the children who were ready for mainstream school were sent to St. Joseph's Convent High School or St. Stanislaus High School.

My sister and I were sent to a boarding school because my father used to hit us and treat us very badly. We lived a very safe and happy life in the boarding and completed our tenth standard from St. Joseph's Convent.

To pursue further studies, I went to Mithibai College, where I completed my H.S.C., working part time and taking care of my family. I worked as an assistant teacher in the pre-primary section at Aseema's Santacruz school. I was very happy to be at Aseema because it reminded me of my teachers who taught us so patiently and lovingly.

After some years, I did the Assistant Montessori course and later completed the AMI Montessori course from Sir Ratan Tata Institute. At present, I am in charge of the pre-primary section at Aseema. I am very grateful to all the Aseema teachers for making my life beautiful by giving me education, love, and support. I am now married and have a happy family and a son. I feel proud to be an educated mother.

I became a teacher because I want to give back to the children what I once received. Aseema has given me education, which has taken me from darkness to light. And not only me, but all the children who have suffered and have gone through pain in their childhood. I believe education is the most powerful weapon that you can use to change the life of a child. It has changed my sister Heena's and my entire life and today we are independent, working, and supporting our family.

At work, I strive to give my best to the children and to create a good and loving environment for each one of them. I know they are deprived of love and care at home. I have now completed ten years of working in the pre-primary section and I feel very happy when I see these children grow. Some of them are now in the ninth and tenth standards.

I feel happiest when I see the smile on a child's face as they learn, and I thank God for Aseema that it has changed my life and many children's lives.

Ramesh Ghayal

Ramesh's parents were construction workers who moved from site to site and so he lived in the home of an elderly Parsi lady, Chhoti, who had taken a great liking to the boy.

It was a couple of years after Aseema had started working at PCMS that Chotti called me one morning to ask if Ramesh could join our classes. At the time, we had too many students and too few teachers and when I hesitated, she pleaded, "Please let him attend the art classes at least." That is how Ramesh came to Aseema at the age of 11. He attended Varsha teacher's art classes, and she immediately recognised his potential.

Ramesh was very well-behaved, which was in sharp contrast to some of our other children, who were terribly mischievous and kept the teachers on their toes. There were instances when some of the naughty ones squeezed their way between the bars of the window of the first-floor classroom and hung outside, which gave their teachers many anxious moments! Ramesh's good behaviour prompted Monika, a young Swiss volunteer, to offer to teach him other subjects as well.

Ramesh had dropped out of the previous school he studied in and was sure that he did not want to get back to formal schooling. We thought differently and felt it was important for him to continue with his education. We also realised that most mainstream schools dampened the enthusiasm and creativity of children and hence looked into different options for Ramesh. We came upon Jeevan Nirwaha Niketan (JNN), a school that followed the NIOS system.

After a lot of persuasion, Ramesh enrolled at JNN. He thoroughly enjoyed his time at the school and charmed many of his teachers. After completing his schooling, we were very keen that he pursue college, but Ramesh had other plans for himself. He underwent many courses in computers and animation, something that had always fascinated him.

All through these years, both when he was at school and later, Ramesh attended Varsha's art classes, first with all the other children and later, individually. Varsha often says, "When I teach Ramesh something, he comes up with something ten times better." Then she would laugh heartily and add, "I often find the roles between teacher and student reversed!" Ramesh learnt rapidly under Varsha and she introduced him to different art techniques, artists, and craftspeople.

He mastered the art of papier mâché, and today makes the most beautiful masks, bowls, and animal figures, which he paints himself. After being introduced to Wycinanki (the Polish art of paper cutting) and Chinese paper cutting, Ramesh started making exquisite paper cuttings as well. Having learnt how to make frames, he sometimes carves and paints the frames into which he inserts the paper cutting, making it a beautiful work of art. His decoupage work is also of high quality and the *barni's* (jars) that he makes are much sought after.

While we would have loved Ramesh to enrol at an art or architecture college, he had other plans for himself.

He was one of the first Aseema children to start earning and inspired many children who had dropped out of school to come back and complete their education. His first mobile phone and bike prompted many school drop-outs to re-enrol! He has done more in getting older children to continue with their education than any amount of coaxing by the teachers.

The concentration with which Ramesh works, and the perfection he attains in all the products he makes is exceptional, which is what makes him such a special boy, and boy is what he will always remain to some of us who have had the pleasure of seeing him grow into adulthood as a fine young man.

Ramesh is now married and has two lovely daughters who also study at Aseema. He has purchased a flat in a distant suburb of Mumbai for his parents and other siblings, which speaks volumes about his sense of responsibility.

A few years ago, he purchased a couple of cars and started an Uber service, which was doing well until the COVID-19 pandemic struck. There has unfortunately been a setback in this business venture, but knowing his tenacity to work hard and overcome all odds, we are confident that he will soon bounce back.

Sunita Gaddam's story in her own words:

I was studying in a municipal school in Bandra in the fourth standard when I joined Aseema. This was in 1998.

At Aseema, I used to attend morning classes at the Chimbai School and go to the municipal school in the afternoon. After a year, I asked my mother if she would like to send me to a private school in Bandra. My mother readily agreed, and I was admitted to St. Joseph's Convent High School. Since the education in my previous school was not good, I had to start all over again and landed in the first standard from the fourth. I had eight other friends from Aseema who enrolled along with me.

It was the best school I'd ever been to in my life! Sister Celestine, the school principal, took extra care of us. She asked all of us to come early to school and would make us have a bath and get ready. Our breakfast and lunch were taken care of by her. Sister Celestine and the others gave us so much love!

After school hours, we continued attending Aseema's Support Centre at St. Stanislaus High School from 4:00 p.m. to 6:00 p.m. At 6:00 p.m. we were served a delicious snack or sometimes even dinner. Since my eight other friends stayed in the same area, we all went to school together and would wait for each other until we all got ready.

I was good at studies, sports, and also in art. I used to always get an 'A' grade and my art would be loved by all. I often got the first prize in drawing competitions that were held in school and sometimes outside. I liked studying and was always curious to know about things. I also worked very hard to get good grades. I have so many certificates and scholarships given by my school—whenever I look at them, it makes me so happy and nostalgic.

But by far, the happiest place to go to was Aseema's Support Centre! It meant fun, *masti*, outings, new learning, along with studies and unconditional love. I'd eagerly wait for the clock to strike 4 o'clock so we could run to Aseema, which was initially at St. Stanislaus and then at St. Joseph's. We had a lot of extracurricular activities like art, music, yoga, dance, judo and theatre. Though there was darkness at home, Aseema gave us light—a ray of hope and never made us feel underprivileged or insecure.

Art classes were held by Varsha teacher every Monday. She'd explain beautifully about the art and about renowned artists like Picasso, Van Gogh, Gond, Warli paintings, and magic paintings and we would paint our hearts out! I used to enjoy painting along with my friends. I loved using oil pastels because shading would be easier to merge, which reflected like a real painting. I'd do more abstract paintings and nature-related art, but wasn't good at drawing human forms. Our paintings would be displayed in different art galleries in Mumbai and every year at the Harmony Show held by Mrs Tina Ambani. I absolutely loved seeing my paintings being bought by people coming to the exhibition, admiring and complimenting us all!

We'd go for so many outings, music and drama concerts and to water parks. The best was going to Redstone Farm in Panchgani. I had so much fun and enjoyed the trip like anything!! Sometimes while going out, Dilbur teacher would come to pick us up and take us in her car. Everyone wanted to sit in her car or go with her. That was the level of excitement when she used to come. We'd feel very happy and shout with glee!! Along with so many other teachers like Zia, Nicola, Tannaz, and Nilofer.

Initially, at the Support Centre, we had Alice teacher. She was very strict, and we all used to get a bit scared of her. But we loved her all the same. She was amazing! Though she never taught me personally, I remember she would trust us with money and give us the responsibility of handling it. Many volunteers also used to come and teach us.

My favourite was Crystal teacher. She'd primarily teach us English and then other subjects as well. I used to be with her most of the time, and everyone used to say I was her favourite student too. Carolyn teacher also taught me a lot.

When I came to the secondary section, a volunteer, Shyama teacher, came into my life and helped me in science, maths, and English. She made me feel I could do better and always guided and motivated me to work hard. She imparted to me so many values and I remember to this day all that she taught me. She focused on developing my personality and instilled in me the importance of education. She is the one who told me that I can score 90% in the SSC board examination. I will always remember her words. Accordingly, I put in a lot of hard work and firmly believed I could do it. Even then, when the results came, and I scored 91%, I couldn't believe it! Then later I realised, that hard work and perseverance pay off!!

I chose to pursue commerce in the twelfth standard and got admission to one of the best colleges in town, Jai Hind College. Initially, I faced a little difficulty with accounts. But then another volunteer, Gitanjali teacher helped me with it and I started doing better. From Gitanjali teacher, I learned that there is life beyond studies and she helped me to develop personally. She was a great mentor and stood by me all the time while I completed my graduation.

Then, after the twelfth standard, I did my Bachelor's in Management Studies and completed my graduation, scoring 78%. It had always been my dream to do an MBA from a recognised institute. Then a miracle happened! Varsha teacher's brother, Ashwin Sir, agreed to sponsor my MBA. I was jumping with joy!!

At that time, campus placements were taking place in my college. This was in the last semester of my third year. So, I went for the aptitude test, which I cleared. I knew nothing about this test but gave my best and got selected. My happiness knew no bounds! I cleared the HR and presentation rounds too and was selected by Wipro to go to Bangalore and complete my Executive MBA and also work with them. Initially, I was hesitant, as I had never lived away from my mother and my family. However, with encouragement given by Ashwin Sir and Gitanjali teacher, I decided to go to Bangalore. They both prepared and arranged everything I needed to make a new beginning in Bangalore and get settled.

I got over my initial hesitation and fear as I always wanted to change my life and give a good life to my parents. There were about 80 students like me who joined Wipro, and hence, the change was made easier. I made new friends and slowly settled down in Bangalore. I worked at Wipro as an HR professional for six years and recently made a change and am now working in HR at Accenture.

I still have a long way to go and want to climb the ladder of success. I am willing to put in any amount of work to get better and better at what I do and also to grow as a person.

Above all, I am very grateful to God for sending all the above-mentioned beautiful people into my life. What I am today is because of their love, encouragement, and support, and I will be grateful to them as long as I live.

Ashish Gaikwad's story in his own words:

Life is a journey, but if you don't have a dream to become something in life, then that journey is meaningless. My journey towards my dream started when I joined Aseema when I was five years old. My mother always tells me that I have only given birth to you, but Aseema is your real mother and that is really true. Aseema put me in St. Stanislaus High School, where I completed my school education. At Aseema, we had other activities such as art, judo, singing, drama, etc. and I was always curious to learn everything, so I took part in all the activities. Occasionally, we used to go to watch good films in the theatres.

In 2007, Amole Gupte (writer and director) volunteered at Aseema and took workshops. We were shown world cinema, and he asked us to write about the films we saw. It was then that I knew I wanted to make a career in filmmaking. After a few years of attending these workshops, I made a short film called *Tahaan* (thirst) and showed it to Amole Sir. He appreciated my work and shared it with his friends. One of them was Subhash Ghai (a well-known Bollywood director). Mr Ghai is also the chairman of Whistling Woods International (a film institute in Mumbai). My film was screened at Whistling Woods when Bollywood was celebrating 100 years of cinema and I was awarded a full scholarship to learn filmmaking there. It was a proud moment for me. I went on to complete a two-year filmmaking course there. I have recently completed shooting a Marathi feature film as a writer and director, and hope it will be released in theatres soon.

As an alumnus, I am very thankful to Aseema for the support given to me over the years. Without them, my journey towards my dreams would never have begun.

Conclusion

The above are stories of only a few of our first batch of students. Many others have also done very well for themselves. Constraints of space prevent me from mentioning them all here. What is particularly heartening is that they continue to have very close ties with their families. Values like honesty, loyalty, gratitude, and humility are ingrained in them. These were the children I was very close to. We were a small organisation then, like a close-knit family. Yes, we called ourselves the Aseema family, and it truly felt like one.

When our student Naushad, aged nine years, passed away on October 7, 2001, we were shocked and grief-stricken. He and a few other friends were playing in a municipal garden and the gate suddenly fell on him, killing him instantly. Naushad was good at sports and a very likeable young boy. We had a little prayer service for him in our classroom at St. Stanislaus, where we put flowers around his photograph and whoever wanted to say a few words did so. This helped the children to grieve, and we were able to talk about death in a way the children would understand, and not be frightened of.

A few years later, we lost little Rifa, who was only six years old, to dengue. The local municipal hospital could not treat her and she was shifted to a private hospital, but did not survive. I last saw her through the glass window in the ICU, a very pretty and dainty little girl. She looked like she was sleeping peacefully. "Please do everything possible to save her," I remember telling the doctor. But it was not meant to be.

We thereafter instituted two scholarships—one in memory of Rifa, who was an exceptionally clever little girl, for academic excellence, and the other for sportsmanship, in memory of Naushad.

To date, many batches of students have finished school and gone to college, some have taken up employment in different fields and some are studying as well as doing part-time jobs. For those who require assistance, Aseema continues to contribute towards their college education.

In 2014, these students came together and formed the Aseema Alumni Association. At its first meeting, they stated that some of them continue to require help from Aseema in the form of financial assistance or teaching them subjects they find difficult in college. Many of them are also interested in giving back and volunteering at the schools or the product division.

Of course, everything has not always been rosy. There have been cases that have been very painful for us, and undoubtedly for the children as well. We can only honestly say that we tried and did everything in our power to give the child a better future. But sometimes, due to some factors, beyond our or perhaps the child's control, we have not been successful.

There was a case of a very sensitive child at Aseema who took to drugs, and despite our best efforts, was unable to give up the habit. Every visit to the rehabilitation centre would end up with him leaving before the treatment could be completed. He would hallucinate and on one occasion, came to our office and threw a stone, smashing the glass window. Fortunately, no one was injured, but we had to take steps to ensure he did not come again to either the office or the school.

It has been a huge learning that we must have patience and perseverance, but also have the wisdom to know when to let go.

As stated in the most wonderful Serenity Prayer:

"God grant me the Serenity to accept the things I cannot change;
Courage to change the things I can;
and Wisdom to know the difference."

36

People Who Helped Make a Difference

"Life's persistent and most urgent question is, 'What are you doing for others?'"

– Martin Luther King Jr.

Over the years, many people have assisted us in our work. Some have given their time, and others have contributed financially. Every donation and any kind of support or even a kind word has motivated us to do more for our children.

In the beginning, apart from Fr. Lawrie who helped us, Anahita Havaldar from the Concern India Foundation informed us that they would be giving us a donation to run the education centre that we proposed starting soon. The donation would enable us to run the centre for a year and we were ecstatic!

Over the years, I have seen how important it is to start small, with whatever is available, work hard, and do everything with a lot of attention to detail, with awareness and love, and things ultimately fall into place. Another thing we have seen is that whenever there is a sincere and genuine need, the universe will ensure that the need is met. The right people will come, the donation will arrive, and things will work out. The person does not have to be the most brilliant, and the donation does not have to be huge—it is the intention and the aspiration that are most important.

There have been many kind and generous donors and though we would love to, it is not possible to mention them all here. Some have been more than donors; they have been so closely associated with our work that we now consider them part of our Aseema family.

The Kundalias

Preeti and Ashok Kundalia are old college friends of mine. We had studied at St. Xavier's College in Mumbai, and a few years after Aseema had been set up, they gave us our first office in Bandra. It was such a blessing! It is a place that all of us who work there love dearly. The administrative work for all our schools happened there until we were too many to be accommodated in that space and had to rent a bigger office. Today, all our documentation, alumni and MCGM work continues to take place at this office.

Their contribution towards attempting to make Aseema self-sustaining has been immense. Preeti and Ashok are major donors and Preeti is also a trustee. Many Aseema paintings adorn the walls of their home and office, and their support and guidance over the years has been invaluable. Their sons, Sambhav and Ravi, are also interested in all that we do at Aseema and I hope and pray that they will continue to support Aseema as their parents have done all these 25 years.

The Kassams

In 2001, I received a call from a friend who was attending a seminar at Bombay University. "Dilbur, there is a lady here who wants to know more about the work at Aseema; please talk to her," she said, and Meenaz Kassam came on the line. "I would like to meet you and understand more about what you do," she said.

We met shortly after that at our office and talked at length about what Aseema did. Meenaz was very interested in knowing all the details and visiting our schools. She lived in Toronto, Canada and taught sociology at the University of Toronto. Her mother lived in Bandra, Mumbai and whenever she visited her mother, she made it a point to also visit us. And so, the association with Aseema grew along with the friendship.

On one of her visits, Meenaz came with her husband, Moe. We all immediately took a great liking to him. Moe asked a lot of questions and always had a calculator with him and if something did not tally, he would grill us, often making us feel like we were being cross-examined! But we liked him enormously and also realised that his questions brought more clarity to what we did. Both Moe and Meenaz, their sons Mikhail and Moez and their nephew, Mehmood Remtulla, have been major and generous donors.

Meenaz has also been on Aseema's Advisory Board for several years. She and Moe now live in Dubai for one part of the year and in Toronto for the other, but they continue to visit Mumbai and attend every advisory board meeting.

Thrity Dolykuka

Soon after Aseema was formed, one of the volunteers at the support centre at St Stanislaus suggested I meet Thrity. "She will be a great help to Aseema," she said. And she certainly was.

I first met Thrity when I was a law student at Government Law College in Mumbai. She was the personal secretary to the eminent jurist, Nani Palkhivala. A group of us had gone to Bombay House, the head office of the Tata Group, to invite Mr Palkhivala to judge a moot court competition at our college. We had no appointment, only a strong desire to have the great jurist visit our college. We were shown into Thrity's office. She was young and pretty and very kind to us. After listening to us, she ushered us into Mr Palkhivala's office and we were on top of the world! Simply to meet the man, who, for all law students, was a legend. He immediately agreed to come to judge the competition, which delighted us even further.

It was many years later that I met Thrity again. As Aseema had no office at the time, Thrity came over to my home one morning with a beautiful bouquet of flowers and said that she would like to volunteer. She was smartly dressed as always and very dignified. When I asked her what she would like to do, she said she would be willing to do anything we needed.

Over the 14 years I knew Thrity, that is what she always did, filled in whenever and wherever the need arose. The hardest and most unpleasant of tasks were performed, without any questions being asked and very willingly.

She loved the Aseema children, and she loved Aseema. She had worked with the House of Tatas for over 30 years, most of the time with Mr Palkhiwala and was fiercely loyal to both. She was equally loyal to Aseema and appreciated the values we stood for. It made her incredibly happy when people appreciated the beautiful art and the quality of our products. She was extremely free and broad in her thinking. "We must appreciate what all NGOs are doing," she would say. "There should be no competition between NGOs. Our goal is only to do good and assist underprivileged children, so where is there room for competition?"

Thrity very much enjoyed going to the exhibitions we were invited to and manning the Aseema stall there. In the early years, she attended every exhibition we had, including our stall at the Harmony Show. Even if the day was long, Thrity would be there early, well before everyone else, and would make sure that the display was proper and that everything was clean and in the right place. She would always stay till the very end, helping with everything and ensuring that we left the place neat and tidy. No task was below her dignity; she would often dust and clean things herself.

In one of the municipal schools where Aseema worked, a classroom had been handed over to us to use, which was in dreadful condition. Old broken furniture had been stored in it for years and it was full of paper and other useless materials. Pigeons had made their home in this frightful mess, and termites had destroyed most of the books and other documents. It was quite a task cleaning it and while the municipal school staff kept a safe distance, not willing to get their hands dirty, Thrity jumped right in. She personally supervised and actively participated in the cleaning of the room to ensure it was ready for use in a few days.

She lived a simple life, enjoyed the simple things and had many interests—reading, embroidery and art and craft. She also attended Taichi classes regularly. She was always very punctual and extremely well-organised. She carried with her a 'portable office' with pens of all colours, pencils, ruler, stapler, punch, pins of all sizes and shapes, glue, measuring tape, everything one would ever need! She was always very polite and courteous to everyone—from a big donor to the simplest villager. When a villager admired a blouse she was wearing, on her next trip to the village, she gave them the blouse, which the villager promptly turned into a sari blouse!

What brought the most joy to Thrity were her visits to Igatpuri. Always ready for adventure, she had readily agreed to conduct the preliminary survey of the villages there. Together with our social worker, Ashok and a volunteer, Sonali, she spent more than 15 days going to the village of Awalkhed and the little hamlets, often on foot as there was no road at the time. They carried a tiffin packed for them by Shukra of the Paramahansa Yogananda Sadhnalaya and shared their simple meal with the even simpler one of the tribal villagers. Thrity often recounted their visit to the villages and hamlets. It had been something that gave her tremendous fulfilment.

The early days in Igatpuri were difficult; we travelled by second-class train and walked to most places. The rickshaw rides were bumpy and there was always the risk of falling out of the overflowing rickshaws! Hours were spent in the scorching summer sun when the land survey and measurement were going on, and there were endless visits to the villager's homes and even their relatives' homes in search of an appropriate site. I sometimes fell ill, got tired and lost hope, but Thrity was like a rock. "This too shall pass," she would often say.

When the day for the purchase of land and registration of the document finally arrived, it was Thrity who accompanied me to the registration office to complete all the legal formalities. Acquiring the land had been a long and arduous process, full of ups and downs.

It was a great relief to know that the land now belonged to Aseema and that we could go ahead with our plan to create a suitable learning environment for the children of the tribal communities.

Immediately after the formalities were over, we went to the Paramahansa Yogananda Sadhnalaya where we had spent so many days, weeks, months and years waiting for this happy day. I remember thanking her for all that she had done and for always having been there. She brushed that aside, saying, "Don't be so silly!"

My greatest regret is that Thrity did not see our education centre once it was built and operational. She had been ill for about two years before she passed away on February 1, 2012. Her kidneys had started failing, and she was advised dialysis, which she initially refused. One thing Thrity did not like was her medicines, and she avoided taking them as much as she could. She continued to enjoy all our office outings—dinner followed by a late-night movie or even an adventurous lunch in the pouring rain at Matheran—she was game for everything and a very good sport.

As Madhumita Ray, another committed volunteer once said, "They don't make people like Thrity anymore." Those of us who knew her still miss her very much and the place she occupied in our office continues to be known as "Thrity's desk". We miss her quiet and thoughtful ways and are happy with the thought that she lived life fully and did what she believed in. She often said, "Life has to go on", and it does, but we continue to remember and miss our 3T!

Alice Francis

Alice was Karen Francis' mother and Karen had been my best friend in school. Karen was a very good student and encouraged me to study hard too. We often studied at each other's homes, which is how I knew Alice well. She would make the most delicious fried masala mackerel which I loved. Karen's father, who was the chief engineer on a ship, often gave me Kraft cheese, which was not freely available at the time, which I also loved.

Alice was a trained Montessori teacher and had taught in a primary school for many years. After retirement, she joined Aseema and was with us all the years we were at St. Stanislaus and St. Joseph's Convent till she left for Australia to be close to Karen.

Alice was quite strict, but she loved the children. They too grew very fond of her. Having no background in education myself, and with no experience of working in a school, I learned a lot from Alice. It was a blessing having someone like her who took complete responsibility for teaching the children.

I missed her sorely when she left for Australia. The news of her passing away brought with it sadness, but also fond memories of the early years. We, the children and I are quite sure that she continues to observe us from wherever she is and is keeping a watchful eye on us to make sure we are doing and behaving well.

Ramesh Kapadia

Ramesh is married to Shweta, who studied architecture with my sister Arnavaz in Mumbai many years ago. He lives in London and has been an Ofsted inspector of schools in the United Kingdom for many years.

When my niece Kamal went to study at Oxford University, Shweta and Ramesh kept a watchful eye on her and she often visited them during her stay in the U.K.. At that time Ramesh set up the Vidya Trust which focused on assisting organisations in India working in education. When he heard about Aseema, he visited us in Mumbai and got so interested in our work that he subsequently visited us every year and encouraged his son, Sujit and colleague, Carol Donoghue, to visit our schools as well. Both Carol and Sujit were also trustees of the Vidya Trust. Carol was also a former Ofsted inspector and like Ramesh, she would observe classes at our schools and give feedback to the teachers and all of us.

Ramesh was one of our earliest donors and was extremely strict with us in the beginning. The teachers in school would tremble whenever I gave them the news that he was visiting. We gradually got used to Ramesh's ways as he got used to ours. The feedback he provided was very useful, and it helped the head teachers, Geeta Subhedar in particular and also Bushra Shaikh, to be more systematic and organised in their work. Geeta, as mentioned earlier, is the education head at our Kherwadi school and Bushra at the Pali Chimbai Municipal School. He took Geeta under his wing when she took over the charge of the Kherwadi Municipal School and provided her with support at every step as the school grew, for which both she and I are extremely grateful to him.

Soli Dastur

Mr Dastur is a very senior and respected lawyer, reputed to be the best tax lawyer in India.

We requested his assistance on several occasions and he has always obliged, giving us legal advice and donating generously to our cause through the Frer Armsolal Charitable Trust formed in his wife's memory.

Mr Dastur was always gracious and patient with us and paid the greatest attention to every detail. He would painstakingly make changes by hand on lengthy documents and go over the same to make sure everything was taken care of. When I shared this with my colleague Snehal, she said, "Make sure you keep Mr Dastur's handwritten notes carefully; they are worth a fortune," such was the esteem in which lawyers hold him.

His daughter, Farahanaaz, visited us whenever he made a donation, and she too was an absolute pleasure to interact with. Later, Farahnaaz was associated with the Mehli Mehta Music Foundation (MMMF), which trained students in Western classical music.

The MMMF has been conducting singing classes for our students for many years now. They have helped greatly in developing the children's English language skills and in teaching them about beat, rhythm and tone.

The 'Singing Tree Concert' organised by the MMMF, is a coveted annual event for students. It is a moment of great pride for both teachers and parents to see the young talented singers perform every year at the iconic National Centre for the Performing Arts (NCPA), together with other students trained by the foundation.

Being Human – The Salman Khan Foundation

One afternoon, many years ago, we received a telephone call in our tiny office in Bandra which was answered by Thrity Dolykuka who volunteered with us at the time. "Dilbur, this is for you," she said and handed me the receiver. "Hi, this is Salman," said the person at the other end and I almost fell off my chair. "Salman Khan, the actor?" I ventured to ask. "Yes, the same," was the reply. "Look, I understand that your organization, Aseema, is running the municipal school in Chimbai, Bandra and I would really like to help." He added, "Why don't you come and meet me."

The next evening I went to his home with Murad Bukhari, a young volunteer, who worked with us and we were enthusiastically greeted by his two dogs, Myjaan and Myson, who took an instant and great liking to Murad. After a long wait, we met Salman and told him about our work at Aseema. "I will ask my sister to visit," he finally said.

The next day, his sister, Alvira Agnihotri, came to our Pali Chimbai Municipal School and we took her around the school and spoke at length about what we did. Soon thereafter, the Being Human Foundation started funding the Secondary Sections of our schools, which they did for nine years, until 2020, when the COVID-19 pandemic struck.

We were also a part of Being Human's 'Real Heroes' campaign in 2014 which created much excitement across our schools. We will always be grateful for the generous support we received from them.

Donors: Corporates and Trusts

Children at the Singing Tree Concert organized by the Mehli Mehta Music Foundation

We have been fortunate to have had corporates, trusts, and individuals who have supported us over the years in our work. Thanks to generous financial contributions from BNP Paribas, Bansuri Trust, Being Human Foundation, Concern India Foundation, Credit Agricole, Dalal Engineering Private Limited, Development Bank of Singapore, GCO Global, HDFC Credila, HSBC, H.T. Parekh Foundation, Lotus Trust, Moet Hennessey, Nivea, Nomura, NRB Bearings, Reliance Foundation, Rustomjee Group, Saint Gobain, Societe Generale, Swiss Re-Insurance Company Ltd., Petronet LNG Limited, Tech Mahindra Foundation, Vidya Trust and Wipro Cares, we have been able to carry on with our work and reach out to many children.

Some of these organisations funded us for a few years (as per their rules of supporting an organisation for three to five years) and some continue to do so. There are so many others who have also contributed, and while it is not possible to mention them all, we are immensely grateful to each and every one of them. It is thanks to their generous support that we have been able to continue our work over the past 25 years. For those corporates and organisations who continue to donate generously, we are hugely indebted. Continuity and stability in our work are critical and these are issues we are still grappling with 25 years later. Educating children is a slow and gradual process, and educating children from marginalised communities is even more so. Hence, continuing support is essential to ensure that the children's learning continues uninterruptedly.

We often hear that an organisation needs to be self-sustaining and we still struggle with that goal. How does an organisation like Aseema, which educates the poorest of the poor without charging a single rupee by way of fees, become self-sustaining? A women's income-generating programme or self-help group may achieve such self-sufficiency at some stage, but how does an education organisation like ours achieve that?

Our attempt to do this with the product division has produced limited results. We are now looking at our Education Training Centre to help generate revenue, but it is still in a nascent stage.

Another question we are repeatedly asked is, "Do you have any plans to scale up?" While we would love to reach out to many more children from marginalised communities, we are convinced that we should only do it if we can ensure quality. Given the nature of our approach, which is so intensive, encompassing not only academics but also co-curricular activities like art, sports, music, gardening, tailoring and also including the children's nutrition and physical and emotional health, it's a very tall order. But one which we sincerely believe in, dream about and continue to strive towards.

Scaling up would need financial resources and committed and competent people. We hope and pray and make every effort to ensure that what started with 18 wide-eyed, playful children will grow to reach out to many more who deserve a better future.

37

Friends of Aseema and Ausbildung, Die Stark Macht

"Unless someone like you cares a whole awful lot, nothing is going to get better. It's not."

– Dr Seuss, The Lorax

Friends of Aseema (FoA)

Mukul Pandya, Executive Director and Editor in Chief of *Knowledge@ Wharton* was very keen to set up a charitable organisation in the US to support Aseema's charitable activities in India. He started working towards setting up a Section 501 (c) (3) organisation there, but the paperwork was cumbersome and the permissions were delayed.

Friends of Aseema was finally set up in New Jersey as a not-for-profit organisation in early 2016, but before a team could come together to work on it, Mukul fell seriously ill and was on medical leave for a long time. As a result, though FoA existed on paper, it did not come to life as an active organisation.

Meanwhile, in 2018, I received an e-mail from Christine Biancheria, whom I had known when I worked with the International Commission of Jurists (ICJ) in the 1990s. Christine had been awarded an international human rights fellowship to work at the ICJ in Geneva, at its Centre for the Independence of Judges and Lawyers (CIJL). She went back after her summer internship to complete her law studies at the University of Pittsburgh, School of Law.

It was almost 24 years later that I received her e-mail. Christine had just given up a thriving legal practice in civil and public interest litigation and decided to catch up with all those she had known in Geneva. I was one of them. She had read about Aseema and was so keen to know more about the organisation that she visited us in Mumbai in early 2019 with her partner Susan. They visited all our schools in Mumbai and Igatpuri and wanted to know every possible detail about our work.

On their return to the US, they met Mukul and actively worked on setting up Friends of Aseema in Pittsburgh. In July 2019, FoA was re-established as a Pennsylvania non-profit organisation and obtained Section 501 (c) (3) status in March 2020, with Christine as its president and Mukul and many others as directors.

In a very short time, Christine was able to spread the word about our work. She would have house parties, talk to the press and do whatever she could to spread awareness. I truly believe that she dreams, thinks and lives Aseema, so passionate is she about the organisation. "I don't know much about fundraising," she would say, "but I'm willing to try to do everything possible." And that she did with love, compassion and tremendous enthusiasm!

She visited Mumbai once again in February 2020 to learn more. This time she met and talked to many of our students, alumni, teachers, the other staff and even visited the community at Bandra Reclamation. She was able to inspire another FoA Director, Robin Tom, to visit and even spend time at our tribal school in Igatpuri.

Once back in the US, she started thinking even more about what could be done to raise funds, and in a very short time, she was able to send us our first donation from FoA. Christine did all this while working as a judicial clerk, providing legal advice and drafting court orders and opinions.

But then COVID-19 struck! And, given its spread and the havoc it created in the US, we thought no further fundraising would be possible there. But Christine was not one to give up easily and got actively involved in our 'Together We Can' campaign. In fact, when the lockdown happened in India in late March, she was one of the first to ask, "What about the children? How are they? Since they do not come to school, what about their meals? What about their parents, who can't go to work?"

FoA was able to collect sizeable funds which, together with what we collected in Mumbai, allowed us to provide groceries to over 1800 of our children's families, totalling almost 10,000 people in the months of April, May, and June.

Christine has the extraordinary ability to get others involved in the work. Her enthusiasm is truly infectious and all of us at Aseema marvel at the speed at which she gets things done. The COVID-19 pandemic did not deter her from distributing brochures and Aseema products to her entire neighbourhood and getting one of her directors to agree to give us a matching grant.

A gardening activity

For us at Aseema it is wonderful to have an organisation like Friends of Aseema supporting us. At times one feels isolated and wonders what the future holds for us. At the beginning of every year, we can only hope that we will be able to raise the required funds. Most people and corporates are reluctant to give funds to build a corpus—a large corpus still remains a dream and the struggle for funds never ends. Friends of Aseema, created solely to support our educational activities, shares our thinking and values. As Christine says, "Aseema is a beacon of what we can achieve when we love without regard to nationality or colour or caste or religion or socioeconomic status. It is a jewel in the world and a model for change everywhere."

AusBildung, Die Stark Macht

AusBildung, die stark macht (educational and vocational training) is a not-for-profit organisation established in Germany. It aims to support Aseema and other similar organisations that work with marginalised children and adolescents and provide them with training for vocational skills, which can be effectively used for career-building.

It was set up by Elizabeth and Benno Lueke, a wonderful couple from Germany who spent a few years in India when Benno was the Managing Director of Thyssenkrupp Industrial Solutions (India) Private Limited and was stationed in Mumbai. Elizabeth was a volunteer at our Santacruz school, where she worked with the little Montessori children.

On their return to Germany, they set up this organisation and are assisting with the vocational training programme in Igatpuri where we currently run the agricultural and gardening training, and also the tailoring programme.

The pandemic slowed down these vocational training programmes, but we are confident that with the support of Elizabeth and Benno, we will be able to build on this very important programme in the coming years.

It is our hope and prayer that similar support groups and initiatives are undertaken for Aseema by like-minded individuals in many other countries, in the years to come.

38

Covid-19

"Learn to stand unshaken amidst the crash of
breaking worlds."

– Paramahansa Yogananda

It started in November-December 2019 when we began getting news of what was happening in Wuhan, China. "Terrible," we thought, "but so far away from us, we really don't need to worry." And we continued with life as before.

Christine Biancheria from Friends of Aseema visited us in February 2020 and spent time in school, meeting with the alumni and visiting the communities. Even when she left two weeks later, wearing a mask for the return journey, the seriousness of the matter had not dawned on us.

Children and teachers came to school as usual as we continued to receive news about the increasing number of cases in Wuhan, then spreading to Europe and the US. By mid-March, the children were asked not to attend school and gradually few and fewer staff attended. A few of us continued to go to the office while Snehal and Arnavaz, at their wit's end, tried to dissuade us. "But I just walk from home to the office in the morning and then back in the evening, so where is the danger?" I protested. And finally came the ultimatum from Arnavaz, "Stop it, you are putting your life, and the others' lives too, at risk." So, on March 20, at 4:00 p.m., I told my colleagues, Annapurna, Shefali and our faithful support staff, Vinayak, "Let's wind up early today. The situation seems to be getting serious," and we left the office, not knowing that we would return only nine months later.

The next day, Prime Minister Narendra Modi spoke to the nation and asked us to observe the '*janata* curfew' on Sunday, March 22.

The public was told not to venture out from 7:00 a.m. to 9:00 p.m. This was simply a prelude to what was to come. On March 24, at 8:00 p.m., he announced a complete 'lockdown' throughout India for the next 21 days. The lockdown started at midnight. While social distancing seemed the only option for the country in its fight against COVID-19, the curfew still came as a shock. It was both sudden and scary.

While the PM assured us that provisions would be readily available so there was no need to panic and hoard, there was still a worry about whether anything would indeed be available. I remember running to my kitchen and thinking, "I can do without vegetables, but need at least rice and dal. I'd better go immediately to the grocery shop and get some." In a panic, I ran to the shop right next to my house. With the shutter half down, the owner was handing provisions to those like me who had rushed there. On the spur of the moment, besides the rice and dal, I added bread and three packets of butter to my list and ran back home. It was all very surreal.

The following Sunday, the Prime Minister asked citizens to show their appreciation and solidarity with all 'Corona Warriors'—doctors, nurses, other medical personnel, sanitation workers and all those involved in providing essential services—by ringing bells or drumming on vessels. I must say it felt very good doing that. For days I had not seen people around me and here I was on my balcony, ringing away on my *thali* and watching my neighbours do the same. It provided a sense of togetherness and hope.

On Sunday, April 5, the PM called upon all 1.3 billion Indians once more, this time to turn off the lights in our homes at 9:00 p.m. for nine minutes and to light lamps, candles or turn on mobile phone torchlights to show our collective determination to beat the coronavirus pandemic.

The lockdown was extended several times—lockdown 1, 2, 3, 4 and so on. Once more, the nation expressed its thanks to the 'Corona Warriors' who were among the worst affected. The army, air force and navy expressed their gratitude by flying over hospitals, bands played and ships lit up after sundown.

After June 1, the curfew lifted ever so slightly, with offices being allowed to work at 10 per cent capacity. Buses, rickshaws and taxis were allowed to ply with minimum passengers. But in a city like Mumbai, it was chaotic and social distancing was simply not observed.

Strangely, one of the first establishments allowed to open were the alcohol shops and the stampede that followed was unbelievable! In Mumbai, they closed once again and reopened a few days later. With the spread of COVID-19 and the number of people being infected and even dying, it was hard to understand the demand for alcohol, but it also went to show where our priorities lay!

Through all this, the migrant workers and daily wage workers continued to be the most affected. With trains coming to a standstill, many trudged home on foot and by bicycle to faraway places like Uttar Pradesh, Chhattisgarh, Ranchi, West Bengal, or wherever their hometowns lay. Some died on the way and the heart-wrenching stories in the media were difficult to digest.

Our students and their families were also very badly affected. Most of their homes are barely 10 x 12 feet. Due to the lockdown, there was no work and so all the family members, numbering five to eight, had to remain within the confines of their homes. Worse still, anyone who stepped outdoors would be beaten up by the police. At one time, news that the army had been called into Mumbai also did the rounds. One mother told our social worker, "This is the first time I am seeing all of us at home together. We usually plan our day such that only some of us are here. It is so crowded now, there is not enough place to even sleep."

Realising that essential groceries and other provisions would be needed by the families of our children, we started the 'Together We Can' campaign. Given the situation, and knowing that everyone faced financial difficulty, we were very unsure of the amount we would raise. Friends of Aseema also supported the campaign and started raising funds in the US. Fortunately, the campaign struck a chord and by June, we were able to provide more than 1,800 of our children's families with essential provisions on two occasions—in April and June. The second time, we also provided an education kit to all the children, as there was no indication of schools reopening.

In Mumbai, we had to provide rooms in all three schools for those in quarantine and it, therefore, seemed unlikely that the children would return to school before the end of the year. Remote learning started initially for the senior classes and then for the younger children, on June 15. Unlike other children, our students do not have laptops or computers at home, which made remote learning a huge challenge. Our community work team, led by Santosh Panigrahi, collected data on the number of parents who had smartphones, as students could learn on these phones. But what about those without cell phones? How would they learn?

In Igatpuri, the situation was even more challenging as most parents did not have smartphones. Fortunately, moving around in Igatpuri was much easier and there were fewer COVID-19 cases than in Mumbai. Distributing learning material, library books and worksheets was still possible there. Fortunately, with the relaxation of the lockdown, our Igatpuri staff was able to come to school in shifts. The open space and environment allowed them to work and follow social distancing norms.

To make matters worse, it was announced that Cyclone Nisarga would hit Mumbai on June 3. Mumbai has not had a cyclone in over a hundred years and given the living conditions in the city, not to mention the rapid spike in COVID-19 cases, we were simply not prepared to handle this;

it would be a catastrophe if it made landfall in Mumbai. The city waited with bated breath. Around 1:30 p.m., news came that the cyclone had slightly shifted course and made landfall at Alibaug, south of Mumbai.

The city experienced only moderate winds, nothing like the 150 kilometres per hour that had been forecast, with almost no damage. We all heaved a sigh of relief, but not for long as we heard that the cyclone was heading north-eastward to Igatpuri! Towards the evening, both Baban Kadam, our social worker, and Rushika Anare, our Assistant Head reported, "We have never experienced such winds in our life. It is absolutely scary!" As there was no electricity, we could not get in touch with our Awalkhed staff on their cell phones, and for some time, we had no idea what was happening. Finally, at almost 11:00 p.m., we received news that while some trees and electric poles had fallen, no major damage had taken place and the storm had moved on.

One morning that June, I spotted my neighbour buying eggs from a vendor who was at her door. Needing some myself, I went in to get a tray. When I got back, the vendor asked, "Are you Dilbur madam?" He pointed to my mailbox, which had my name on it. "Namaste, my son has studied in the Aseema school and is now in college." He went on to add, "He is the only boy in our community who speaks good English."

"What is your son's name?" I asked. "Niyaz," he replied, "everyone in my hometown knows Aseema, as my son has done so well at your school! I am really happy to meet you."

He seemed so pleased that for a while, I forgot all about COVID-19 and Cyclone Nisarga, which had made the past few months one of the most stressful periods of our lives, and visualised how happy Niyaz and his father must feel whenever they visit their hometown in Uttar Pradesh.

39

Remote Learning

"See nothing, look at nothing but your goal,
ever shining before you.
The things that happen to us do not matter, what we become
through them does.
Each day, accept everything as coming to you from God. At night,
give everything back into His hands."

– Sri Gyanamata

With the pandemic came the challenge of teaching the students from home. As the number of cases in Mumbai rose daily, the schools that had shut down in March continued to remain so. By June 2020, the number of cases in Mumbai was frighteningly high, and as the lockdown rules eased and the Unlock-Phase 1 started, the number shot up even higher. Our teachers and other staff continued to work from home, but the question now was how would we teach the children after June 15, which is the regular date of schools reopening.

A certain amount of teaching had happened in April on WhatsApp, but that was without much preparation. The year-end examination, which is usually in March-April, had not been held, while the SSC examination for the students of Grade 10 had taken place. All students, from Grades 1 to 8, are automatically promoted to the next class no matter how they fare in the final examination. Hence, in June, all the children were promoted to the next class. Fortunately, we were able to do some planning during the May vacation and started working on what we would do from June. We realised that many of our teachers did not have laptops or computers at home, so those had to be organised first. Fortunately, we were able to shift many of the computers from school, as well as the spare computers from our office, to our teachers' homes. Some donors had given us their old computers and laptops only a couple of months earlier and these were a great help at this time.

That took care of our teachers' needs. "Now, what do we do for our children?" we asked ourselves. "Would they be able to study in their small homes? What about the distractions all around them? Did their parents have smartphones? What was the internet connection like? What about data plans? How many of them would leave for their villages?"

While our community work team was distributing essential provisions to the families, they collected and compiled this information throughout April and May. The information they collected showed that in Mumbai, 70% of families had at least one smartphone per family. In Igatpuri, only 53% of families had one smartphone per family. The only way to reach out to the children and ensure that they learned was by using these phones.

After talking to the parents, we realised that they were very keen to continue with the children's education. Those planning to leave for their villages told our social workers, "We have no choice but to leave. It is dangerous for us to live in this community, as there are many COVID-19 positive cases. But we will ensure that our children do their lessons on the mobile, so please do send them to us." Then they added, "And we will return to Mumbai and to school, once everything is normal."

And so, we started the 'Back to School' campaign, asking people to donate their old smartphones or Rs. 6,300 for a new phone. The 'Together We Can' campaign for distributing essential provisions to our children's families had been such a success that we were hopeful for this too. Some people donated, some people helped to spread the word, while others gave us lots of encouragement.

We also struggled with how our teachers would prepare the remote learning lessons. There was a lot of trial and experimentation—initially on WhatsApp and slowly moving to Google Classroom and Google Meet, which are much better for learning. The teachers (and all of us) had to learn so much and so fast! Teaching and learning from home were a Herculean task. Teachers quickly prepared lesson plans and teaching aids that would help the children learn through these remote classes. Our trainers gave crash courses to the teachers on how to conduct classes online, and the teachers showed the children how to attend classes and do their homework and assignments. It was probably the most difficult time of their lives, but our teachers and all our staff gave it their 100% and we are eternally grateful to them.

When we saw the first few classes that were posted, we were quite happy. And the children's joy at seeing their teachers again was heart-warming! Both children and parents showed much interest and enthusiasm and dived into the work given to them by the teachers. One of our student's grandmothers learnt to read and write together with her granddaughter in Grade 1. "The teachers at Aseema have shown me how to read as well as how to teach my granddaughter," she said, her eyes sparkling with happiness. At the age of 70, she was the oldest student in class but had the same insatiable curiosity as the rest of the six-year-olds.

A senior teacher at Aseema shared this: "I have now learnt not to take things for granted and to value the small things in life. Most of us teachers would never have dreamt we would be conducting remote learning classes. Our jobs and the way we conducted our classes, interacting with our students face-to-face, were all taken for granted. I miss seeing my students' faces light up when a concept is grasped, or when they know the answer to a question. Remote learning has helped us enhance our computer skills to a great extent, something which might not have happened in normal times, more so as we were very comfortable with the normal way of teaching. The positive part of this pandemic is that it has made us take stock of our priorities and forced us to get creative. We have realised what is important to us and taught us to appreciate what we have. Things might not go the way we planned, but we can recreate plans to fulfil our dreams."

With the pandemic also came financial difficulties. Each one of the 23 years prior to the pandemic was a struggle for funds. This year, we realised, would be much tougher. "Get ready to face a 50% cut in donations" was the advice given to me by a long-time Aseema well-wisher.

"Are our regular donors going to support us this year?" was the question on our minds. "Most corporate social responsibility (CSR) funding has gone for COVID-19 relief and the Prime Minister's Covid Fund" was the news our donor relations team kept getting. In April, a major donor informed us that he was unable to give us anything this year. No cut or deduction, but absolutely nothing. So much had happened in the past few weeks that it did not even come as a shock. Only a sense of disappointment at being so vulnerable. We had no choice but to slash the budget to a bare minimum. The most painful part was introducing pay cuts. But it had to be done. We did it in the fairest manner possible and realised it was time to look after everyone, to try and keep everyone together. We believed it was our goal, ever shining before us, that would not only keep us together but help us get through this difficult time—no matter how long it would last.

Everyone understood and remained steadfast and solid. "We are in this together and we will emerge victorious" was the general message. And then our Igatpuri staff sent this message, *"Yadi iss mahamari mein bhi apko apki salary mil rahi hai toh yakin rakhiye aap duniya ki sabsey bharosemand sansthao mein sey eik me kaam kar rahe hai. Uska saath kabhi ne chodna."* (If you are receiving a salary even in this pandemic, you can be sure you are working for one of the most trusted organisations in the world. Do not ever leave it.)Despite the gloom all around, on reading this, the sun seemed to shine brightly.

40

Beauty without Boundaries 2020

"With this faith, we will be able to hew out of the mountain of despair, a stone of hope."

– Martin Luther King Jr.

With the uncertainty in obtaining donations, we realised that we needed to do something different. I was regularly in touch with Christine and Mukul from Friends of Aseema at this time and Mukul came up with this novel idea of having an online art auction.

The children at Aseema and our alumni had created some beautiful paintings sitting in their tiny homes, which they regularly shared with their teachers, and we had built up a sizeable collection of their art.

Mukul introduced Christine and me to Grace Cho, the CEO of Artrepreneur, an online platform for visual arts. Grace was enthusiastic and dynamic and went through the children's art with great interest. Soon, Artrepreneur, Friends of Aseema, and Aseema embarked on a global online art auction called 'Beauty Without Boundaries 2020'.

It took about four months of regular meetings and a lot of work to put up this auction. Owing to the time difference between the US and India, we sometimes worked late into the night, but everyone did it with enthusiasm and great interest. Mukul's daughter, Tara, helped enormously in uploading the art and write-ups on the Artrepreneur website and setting it all up with Steve and Rob from Artrepreneur. The Aseema auction team, consisting of Reema, Asmita, Gargi, Meeti and Sarah, worked tirelessly to make sure that all the information from our side was sent on time. Grace chaired all our weekly meetings and drove us to meet targets and timelines.

It went live in October and 21 beautiful paintings were auctioned. Videos of the children talking about themselves and their art were put up alongside the paintings, which garnered a lot of interest. To make the event even more interesting, eminent professionals, artists, celebrities, and business icons each donated their time to the highest bidders in 15-minute online conversations. These included artists Anjoli Ela Menon, Senaka Senanayake, Al Gury, Liz Grimaldi, and Vanessa German; authors Shashi Tharoor and Amish Tripathi; actors Priyanka Chopra, Nick Jonas, and Aamir Khan; film director Danny Boyle; astronaut Terry Virts; educators Dr Jerry Wind and Navin Valrani; business icons Kate Johnson and Nitin Rakesh; fashion designer Anita Dongre; area director of the Taj Group, Karambir Kang; and Joanne Rogers, wife of legend Fred Rogers, the American TV host.

Each of these persons graciously gave their time and we will always be grateful to them, as we are to all those who participated in the auction and bought the beautiful art. We had never done anything like this before and it was a huge learning for everyone. Since this was all done at the height of the pandemic and during the lockdown in India, we could not even meet one another.

Each of us sat in our respective homes and met online every Friday evening at 7:00 p.m. to share what we had done during the week and to plan for the next. What would have normally taken six months to accomplish was done in a record four months, thanks to excellent teamwork and Grace's strict deadlines. Of course, there were a few hiccups and challenges, but we were so charged with wanting to do something meaningful and beautiful at such a challenging time that no one really minded.

Not only did the auction raise substantial funds despite a COVID-19-depressed economy, but it reached over five million people in 40 countries. Many people told us that it provided a ray of hope amidst the despondency all around.

And the sun shone even brighter.

41

Technology and Other Opportunities

"If we teach today's students as we taught yesterday's, we rob them of tomorrow."

– John Dewey

Technology

Much has changed since we set up our first computer lab at PCMS. It was a room where 20 computers were installed and the children learned the basics of Word and Paintbrush. In 2011, we embarked on a project with Sri Aurobindo Society and HP and introduced 'Project Ringtones' where students enrolled in after-school classes. Here, our young programmers, with the help of software such as Scratch and Movie Soup, developed games under teacher Gargi Dutta's watchful eye.

Then, as we took on more schools, computer labs were set up in each one, even at our school in Igatpuri, which is in the remote village of Awalkhed. Here, there are days when we do not have electricity, especially during the monsoon, and initially, we were very apprehensive when we set up the computer lab, wondering how it would work. There was only one thing we knew for sure that the children in these remote villages should not be left behind. They needed to be given the same opportunities as children in the cities. And once again, teacher Gargi, who was now in charge of IT, sprang into action and ensured, not only that the lab was set up but also that internet connectivity was available. At first, it was sporadic and quite erratic but now, as our IT team has grown, and with guidance from the technical IT in-charge, Jayant D'Silva, our computer labs and IT infrastructure have improved considerably.

Physically returning to school after almost two and a half years of the pandemic was a truly joyful experience for all the children, teachers and the entire staff. We also realised that so much more is possible with technology. The way we learn has changed quite dramatically.

Today, with smartphones being given to almost all the children (at least one phone per family) and laptops given to the majority of Grades 9 and 10, we are ready for a more blended learning approach and are experimenting with the 'flipped classroom' model. We try to make the best use of class time so that students can undertake activities that involve higher-order thinking in class. Many of our teachers prepare and send information to the students before class so they come prepared for the activities and spend their time in class discussing them.

But even as we introduce more IT in our classrooms and in our offices, we sincerely believe that onsite learning in schools cannot be replaced. The physical contact with the teacher and other children, the bond that develops between child and teacher and between colleagues is of the greatest importance, and the challenge lies in achieving the perfect balance between the two – onsite and online.

Given our education approach, with its emphasis on co-curricular activities and value education, onsite interaction is all the more important and often, absolutely necessary. Also, given the living conditions of many of our children, online interaction is sometimes not an option at all.

Other Opportunities

Fortunately, we have been able to give our children many opportunities that they may not have had otherwise. This is thanks to our generous and thoughtful donors who have organised events and trips that our children have thoroughly enjoyed.

In the earlier chapters, we have seen the exposure our children have received through the art exhibitions we participated in. In sports, too, they attended several IPL cricket matches, and in 2014, three of our students were even taken to an IPL cricket match in Dubai.

Ritika Agarwal had this to say about her trip: "I was very fortunate to get selected among many students to go to Dubai. I was so excited that I was going to fly for the first time. My first international trip, wow! My family members came to drop me off at the airport. I couldn't believe I was really going to Dubai.

"It was April 24, 2014. We boarded the plane and when our flight took off, I was a little scared, but after some time I felt I was flying in a cotton candy world. We reached Dubai International Airport in about three hours. We went to Hotel Oberoi from the airport. At the hotel, I couldn't believe I was standing in front of Rohit Sharma, the Captain of the Mumbai Indians team. Nita Ambani ma'am also came in. After meeting them, we had dinner, went to our room and fell asleep.

"The next morning as we were having breakfast, we were surrounded by IPL players. We were staring at them and not interested in our breakfast. We then went to see the dolphin show and visited the Dubai Garden. We had a lot of fun there.

"The next morning, we had a grand celebration in honour of the whole IPL team. The Aseema students put up a splendid performance for them. During lunch, I was sharing the table with cricket players like Lasith Malinga, Harbhajan Singh, Sachin Tendulkar, and Pollard!

"Finally, it was the day of the IPL match—RCB versus Mumbai Indians. We cheered for our Mumbai Indians team. The stadium was huge and packed with people. On our last day, we were taken on a tour around Dubai. We saw the Burj Khalifa—this beautiful building can be seen from space also. We then visited the Dubai Mall.

"When we returned, we had a surprise in our rooms. Nita ma'am gifted each one of us a box of assorted chocolates. In the evening, a couple who stayed in Dubai (Aseema advisors, Meenaz and Moe Kassam) came to meet us. We conversed a lot and had dinner with them. The next morning, we departed for Mumbai. Before we left, we were all given Sachin Tendulkar's especially gifted bats. Truly, this was a trip that I will cherish forever."

Then, in 2018, thanks to a major donor, eight of our students went to Yokohama, Japan, to attend the Rugby World Cup semifinal match. It was a thrilling experience for them, going all the way to Japan, and interacting with Japanese and other students from all over the world. Once back home, they could not stop talking about all the places they had visited, the people they had met, the food they had eaten and all that they had learnt.

Namdeo Kevhari, who studies at our Igatpuri school, shared his experience in Japan:

"I am a student from Aseema's Bal Shaikshanik Kendra in Igatpuri. I was so happy to join the group that was visiting Japan to witness the Rugby World Cup.

"I had never been to an airport. Neither had I seen an aeroplane at close quarters, let alone travel in one. This was an exciting new experience for me. I watched planes land and take off. Later, an important person took my suitcase and gave me a card. On asking, I was told that it was my boarding pass and that my suitcase would be kept safely in the belly of the plane along with the other passengers' luggage.

"We went first to Hong Kong and then to Japan. Our plane was big and wonderful, with many rows of seats. I settled excitedly in my seat, watched cartoons, and played video games on the computer fixed in front of my seat. In Hong Kong, we changed planes for Japan. When we arrived in Japan, I was surprised to see that everything was so different. A friendly lady met and welcomed us. She helped us onto the bus that took us to our hotel in Yokohama. I liked the showers, but I did not like taking a bath at night before dinner. I prefer the Indian system of bathing in the morning. I enjoyed the dinners of rice, fish, and chicken.

"On the first day, all the international students introduced themselves to each other. I met and befriended many students who had come from different countries to attend the event. However, understanding their different languages was a very big challenge for me.

"I made many friends at Yokohama Junior High School. The students taught us to speak and write a few words in Japanese. They also taught us calligraphy. The school was very clean, and I was amazed to learn that the students themselves were responsible for the cleanliness of their school. The medium of education was Japanese.

"I was thrilled to learn new rugby skills from different international rugby players who also practised a little with us. The pure gold World Cup trophy was on display in the school for us to see. I was fortunate to be close enough to touch this hallowed trophy.

"Watching the semifinal match between New Zealand and England in the stadium was a most wonderful experience.

"The aquarium visit was another amazing experience. The penguins and other colourful fish were delightful to watch. The dolphins entertained the group with their dancing. The sea parade kept us glued to the performance.

"The farewell programme required each student group to sing a song, enact a skit, make a speech, or put up a performance. Our group made the human pyramid and explained its significance. We said goodbye to all the friends we had made. It was an emotional time, and I wondered if we would ever meet again.

"I will never forget this experience as long as I live. In my wildest dreams, I never thought I would visit a foreign country. I want to say a big thank you to Societe Generale for giving me this opportunity. I am also grateful to my teachers for their support, encouragement and care. I, on my part, promise to implement all that I have learnt in whatever way I can."

42

Twenty-Five Years Later

*"Everything about the future is uncertain, but one thing is sure.
God has already arranged all our tomorrows. We have only to
trust Him."*

The first students 25 years later – all grown up and mature

Running three schools in Mumbai and one in Igatpuri has brought
with it a sense of fulfilment and gratitude. That's not to say there has
been no heartache. There are still doubts and uncertainties that arise—
some of these arise from internal matters: staff leaving for better
opportunities, their own goals changing or inability to withstand the
pressure that the work brings. Sadder still is when one has asked staff
to leave as they have not been able to abide by the values Aseema
stands for.

There is always sadness in parting. And it has usually been my job to
undertake this difficult task. While I try to work things out as much as

I can, I have finally learnt that change is necessary, and it brings about greater growth, both at an individual level and also for the organisation.

I try to reconcile with this by building a solid, stable organisation. The stability of key staff is necessary, but in today's scenario, people always seem to be moving. Two to three years in an organisation is considered too long. When I asked one young girl who had come for a job interview why she changed jobs so frequently, she replied calmly, "If you don't change jobs every year, you are considered a failure." Times have certainly changed!

Then there are uncertainties regarding funding. Aseema started with each of us trustees contributing Rs. 5,000 (USD 66). The first donation from the Concern India Foundation enabled us to educate 18 children for almost a year, along with donations in kind from other well-wishers. Today, with more than 9,000 children to educate, feed, provide medical help whenever needed, and maintain our Igatpuri property, the budget is much larger. God has been kind to us and while we do not have huge reserves, He always provides what we need.

The Aseema office is very small but cosy and comfortable and was donated by one of our very generous donors. Only recently, about 20 years after occupying it, thanks to another kind donor, we could afford the luxury of air-conditioning it. I sat in this office together with our donor relations, finance and HR teams and our office administrator for 20 years. Every available space in the office was used and when prospective candidates came for interviews with HR and there was no place available, they sat in the garden. We all love this office which, considering the time we spent there, became our second home.

However, in these days of mushrooming 'professional' NGOs, many people prefer fancier, more 'corporate-looking' offices. As we tried to streamline and strengthen our work, this became a challenge we had to face and remedy.

As we grew, our office staff was spread across three locations—the one mentioned above at Josephine Apartments, our product division at Khar, and our dear friend Nita's house at Santacruz. This led to delays and many other administrative hurdles, so finally in May 2019, we rented a lovely place at Ranwar Village in Bandra, which was much bigger and could accommodate most of us.

All of us finally being in the same place made work easier and more efficient. It was also a pleasure having more space to move around and having a dining room to meet for lunch. Most importantly, we finally had our own toilet on the premises after having had to share a toilet outside our office with our neighbours!

Many thought that with corporate social responsibility becoming the new catchword and 2% of profits being given to NGOs for their work, funds would be readily and easily available. This has not always been the case, and the struggle for funding continues.

As the number of children increases every year, so does the number of staff. New projects are undertaken and we need to keep pace with technology. Given the increase in the cost of living, people need to be paid better. They also need to be motivated and encouraged all the time, and it is critical to reward good performers.

The problems we face with some of the children—ill health, abuse within the family, lack of interest in education—we take in our stride and do our best to overcome. Teachers and staff at Aseema go well beyond the call of duty; many of them truly give of themselves, spending time with the children beyond their normal working hours and interacting with parents to solve difficult problems.

The issues we continue to face with the MCGM can be tiring, and at times, downright exasperating. Sometimes the heads appointed by the MCGM at the schools we run show little or no interest in understanding our approach to education. Aseema has never claimed to be an organisation that has promised to produce only doctors, engineers and lawyers. We have never said that our goal is only to send our students to the Indian Institute of Technology (IIT) or the Indian Institute of Management (IIM). If they do secure admission to any of these institutions, that is a bonus, but it is certainly not our reason d'etre.

The odds against our children are tremendous. Having such difficult circumstances, we consider it a wonder that our children come to school regularly and learn as well as they do. We celebrate all the little battles won, which mean so much to our young ones.

Aseema's goal is to make every child reach their true potential. It is for this reason that we expose them to art, music, sports, and judo, and try to spend as much time on these activities as we do on language, maths, science, history, etc.

A science experiment in progress

It would be far easier for our teachers to simply get the children to memorise their textbooks, copy from the blackboard and reproduce this in the examinations. They may get higher grades and better marks in the final SSC board examinations. But this is not why we started Aseema in the first place, and it is not true education. While giving the child an education that will help him or her procure a job is important, it is not the only goal.

If true education is building character, then it is our duty to expose our little ones to the values we expect them to live up to. We believe it is far more important that the child grows up to be a caring and compassionate adult. To be an adult who is truthful and honest. An adult who respects and is thoughtful of others and thinks and acts responsibly towards their community and the universe at large.

To live such a life, it is important that the child internalises these values. We live in a world where we see increasing intolerance, indiscipline, and corruption all around us. This makes living these values more difficult, but all the more important.

The child can only learn these values from an adult who is living them. This brings us to the even more difficult task of surrounding the child with adults who not only talk about truth, honesty, care, compassion and respect but also put these values into practice. This is what we struggle with as we continue to reach out to more children.

We spend a large amount of resources, both financial and human, in training our teachers in Aseema's approach to education. Our training team works tirelessly to prepare manuals that take the best from SSC textbooks and books from other boards and educational philosophies. The activity-based learning that we have developed makes learning a joy for the students and helps them remember what they have learnt for life, not only for the next examination.

For the past few years, we have been training the teachers of a school in Kanpur—the Amin Public Inter College, which is also a school for children from marginalised communities. More recently, we started training teachers of a school in Lucknow, Unity College and also did an assessment of two schools in Ranchi.

It is our hope that more schools will see the value in this approach and will want to replicate it in their schools. It is an approach that is suitable for all children, but especially for the poorest of the poor who are so deprived of quality education and who deserve much, much better.

As one of our alumni who has just finished her college education, put it:

"There is a difference between education and quality education. I would say that what I received at Aseema was quality education. We had very good teachers and facilities and had exposure to a lot of art and sports and other extracurricular activities. When you don't know where you have to go and when someone guides you, then you really get hope that you can achieve something in life. It's like you are in a family. We are so free to come and speak to our teachers, even after we have left school and they are so very understanding. You know that if you are in trouble, they will come to help you out and this is something which is beyond boundaries."

As mentioned earlier, Aseema is a Sanskrit word that means no boundaries, no limits. As we strive to provide the finest education to the poor and to reach out to many more children, we hope and pray that we can keep on keeping on – guiding, encouraging, and supporting our children to power their dreams and change their lives.

Epilogue

It has been a long, yet extremely fulfilling journey.

A journey difficult to put down in words. The myriad experiences and emotions we have navigated over the last 25 years are so hard to describe. There have been many moments where our work has been encouraged, lauded, and cheered on enthusiastically. And there have been moments when we have faced discouragement, disappointments, and even failure. Whenever faced with the latter, I am thankful that I have always found many well-wishers and supporters who have given me the strength to stand up and carry on.

While this is a narrative put down by one individual, it is a culmination of the hopes, dreams, generosity, kindness, and fortitude of many.

When I started writing this book, I wondered if I would remember all that had happened over 25 years. Surprisingly, it came back like a flood. But there is so much to do at Aseema that I took many breaks in between writing to finish the entire narrative. Now that it is done, I would like to thank all those who assisted with this book.

To the reader, you are one of the many that I thank from the bottom of my heart. Thank you for giving us the strength to continue working towards our mission of educating our children and our future.

To the donors, who believe in our cause and support us year after year, many thanks—we would not be able to do what we do without your encouragement and generous contributions.

To our trustees and advisors, for your guidance and unconditional help.

To our teachers, administrators, social workers, counsellors, support, and the entire Aseema staff, for the care, compassion, and respect you give to our children, I am eternally grateful.

To my brother and sister, for being there for me always and at all times.

To my nieces Zia and Armeen, for motivating me to write the book, for going through the early manuscript and for your numerous suggestions.

To my dear friends, Carol Donoughue and Danesh Bharucha for all your help with the editing.

To my close friend of many years, Mukul Pandya, for encouraging me to finish the book, editing it and giving advice on improving it.

To Haley Surkatha, who interned at Aseema, for the thoughtful additions to the script—they make the book so much more meaningful.

To Delnaz Mistry, for going over the book one more time.

To Kaira Master, for designing the cover of the book and for your help in placing the illustrations.

To Ashish Upadhaya, for painstakingly looking over the final edit.

To Joeanna Fernandes, for her meticulous editing, and Rachita Raisinghani, for her help with the publishing.

To Ashish Gaikwad and his friend Vicky Thorat, for the wonderful illustrations that have made the book come alive.

To Gargi Dutta, who sifted through thousands of photographs collected over the years that made it possible to do the illustrations.

To Sabina Talpade, for carefully going through the manuscript several times and ensuring that every change was incorporated. I thank you for your patience and understanding.

To Bhaswati Mukherjee, Fali Nariman, Indra Munshi, and Rafiq Dada, for their help through all the difficult situations.

To Alice Francis, Percy Ghandy, Shyama Kulkarni, and Thrity Dolykuka, who are now, I am sure, in a better place—thank you for all that you did for Aseema and its children.

To Punit and Bhagubai, for being my biggest supporters, through thick and thin, in Igatpuri.

To my dearest friends, Snehal, Neela, Jyotsna and Mohini, for providing a shoulder to cry on whenever it was needed.

To Notion Press, for ensuring this book sees the light of day.

And finally, many, many thanks to all those who have been with me on this most amazing and fulfilling journey. None of it would have been possible without your help.

God bless you all.

* * *

Ithaka

When you set out for Ithaka
Ask that your way be long
Full of adventure, full of instruction...
Have Ithaka always in your mind
Your arrival there is what you are destined for
But don't in the least hurry the journey
Better it last for years
So that when you reach the island
You are old
Rich with all you've gained on the way
Not expecting Ithaka to give you wealth
Ithaka gave you the splendid journey.

—C.P. Cavafy

How You Can Help

Alone we can do so little, together we can do so much.

People often believe that their individual contributions may not bring about significant change, but it is these small efforts that have helped us move mountains. I hope that reading about our journey has inspired you to become a part of our family. There are many ways in which you can assist us in our mission:

- Help spread awareness about our work and mission amongst your network of family and friends; become our strongest advocate and our ambassador.
- Refer us to your organisation and create awareness for Aseema at your workplace.
- Give us some of your time and expertise in areas such as teaching our students, training our staff, assisting in developing teaching aids, marketing our products, social media marketing, content creation, and more.
- Assist us in our quest to become self-sufficient by considering Aseema products for your gifting requirements.
- Volunteer for career talks and career readiness sessions, which go a long way in assisting our senior students and alumni to become job-ready.
- Assist our placement cell with alumni placements in your organisation.
- Set up an Aseema support group in your country.

If you would like to know more about how you can associate with us, do visit https://www.aseema.org/get-involved/ or https://www.aseema.org/make-a-difference/

If you'd like to share your thoughts and ideas with me, do write to contact@aseema.org

I would love to hear from you.

About the Author

Circa 1995. Dilbur Parakh, a young lawyer with the International Commission of Jurists (ICJ) in Switzerland, made a bold decision. She decided to leave her secure job and a comfortable existence to embrace her true calling – serving the underserved back home in India.

Dilbur's journey from championing women's rights during her years at SNDT Women's University to her stint with the Union for Civil Liberty in Thailand and finally as Legal Officer for Asia and the Pacific at the ICJ, fuelled her passion for meaningful change at the grassroots level.

Alongside her friends, Snehal Paranjape and Neela Kapadia, she founded Aseema—a Mumbai-based NGO with a profound vision: to provide high quality, holistic, value based education to children from marginalised communities.

As Founder and Chairperson, she has fearlessly guided Aseema from very humble beginnings to what it is today. Her unwavering dedication and determination have shaped the organization, one student and one school at a time.

Within these pages, witness Dilbur Parakh's indomitable spirit and journey in her own words. A woman propelled by the belief that quality education unleashes limitless potential and transcends all barriers, her tireless efforts have helped shape a world where the dreams and aspirations of children are not curtailed by their circumstances.